The Cold War

The Cold War dominated international relations for 45 years. It shaped the foreign policies of the United States and the Soviet Union and deeply affected their societies. Hardly any part of the world escaped its influence.

David Painter provides a compact and analytical study that examines the origins, the course, and the end of the Cold War. His overview is global in perspective and focuses on the interaction of international rivalries and national politics and policies. In addition to the geopolitical rivalry between the United States and the Soviet Union that was at the center of the Cold War, he examines such important issues as:

- changes in the global distribution of power
- the dynamics of the arms race
- ideological divisions within and among nations
- the evolution of the world economy
- the political and economic transformations of the Third World

The Cold War gives a concise, original, and interdisciplinary introduction to this international state of affairs, covering the years between 1945 and 1990.

David S. Painter is Director of Graduate Studies in History in the School of Foreign Service at Georgetown University, Washington, D.C.

The Making of the Contemporary World
Edited by Eric Evans and Ruth Henig
University of Lancaster

The Making of the Contemporary World series provides challenging interpretations of contemporary issues and debates within strongly defined historical frameworks. The range of the series is global, with each volume drawing together material from a range of disciplines – including economics, politics and sociology. The books in this series present compact, indispensable introductions for students studying the modern world.

The Cold War

An international history

David S. Painter

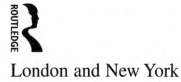

London and New York

First published 1999
by Routledge
11 New Fetter Lane, London EC4P 4EE

Simultaneously published in the USA and Canada
by Routledge
29 West 35th Street, New York, NY 10001

© 1999 David S. Painter

Typeset in Times by
J&L Composition Ltd, Filey, North Yorkshire
Printed and Bound in Great Britain by
Clays Ltd, St Ives plc

British Library Cataloguing in Publication Data
A catalogue record for this book is available from the British Library

Library of Congress Cataloging in Publication Data

Painter, David S.
  The Cold War : an international history/David S. Painter.
    p.   cm.–(The Making of the contemporary world)
  Includes bibliographical references and index.
    1. Cold War. 2. World politics–1945– I. Title. II. Series.
  D843.P25   1999
  909.82—dc21   98–49205
                                                           CIP

ISBN 0–415–19446–6 (hbk)
ISBN 0–415–15316–6 (pbk)

Contents

Abbreviations

CENTO	Central European Treaty Organization, the successor to the Baghdad Pact
CIA	Central Intelligence Agency
DRVN	Democratic Republic of Vietnam (this was North Vietnam)
EEC	European Economic Community
ICBM	Intercontinental Ballistic Missile
INF	Intermediate-Range Nuclear Forces
IRBM	Intermediate-Range Ballistic Missile
MAD	Mutually Assured Destruction
MIRV	Multiple Independently targetable Re-entry Vehicle
MRBM	Medium-Range Ballistic Missile
NATO	North Atlantic Treaty Organization
OAS	Organization of American States
OPEC	Organization of Petroleum Exporting Countries
PRC	People's Republic of China
SEATO	South East Asia Treaty Organization
SDI	Strategic Defense Initiative
SLBM	Submarine-Launched Ballistic Missile
SVN	State of Vietnam (this was South Vietnam)
UAR	United Arab Republic

Maps

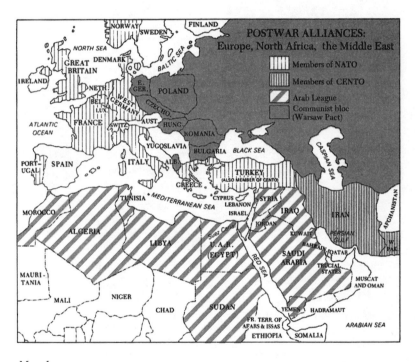

Map 1

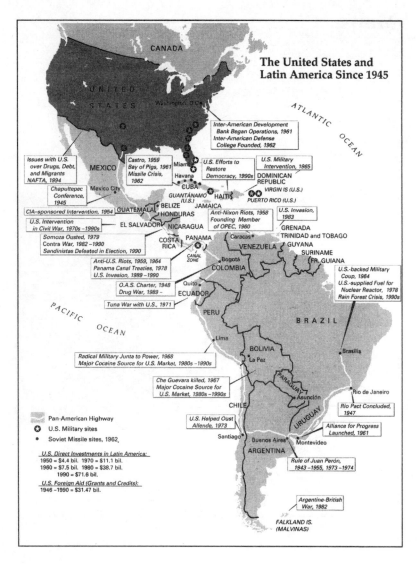

The United States and
Latin America Since 1945

CANADA

UNITED STATES

Washington D.C.

ATLANTIC OCEAN

Inter-American Development
Bank Began Operations, 1961
Inter-American Defense
College Founded, 1962

Issues with U.S.
over Drugs, Debt,
and Migrants
NAFTA, 1994

MEXICO

Castro, 1959
Bay of Pigs, 1961
Missile Crisis,
1962

Miami

Havana

U.S. Efforts to
Restore
Democracy, 1990s

U.S. Military
Intervention, 1965

DOMINICAN
REPUBLIC

Chapultepec
Conference,
1945

Mexico City

CUBA

VIRGIN IS (U.S.)
PUERTO RICO (U.S.)

GUANTÁNAMO
(U.S.)

HAITI

CIA–sponsored Intervention, 1954

GUATEMALA

BELIZE

JAMAICA

U.S. Intervention
in Civil War, 1970s –1990s

HONDURAS

EL SALVADOR

NICARAGUA

Anti-Nixon Riots, 1958
Founding Member
of OPEC, 1960

U.S. Invasion,
1983

Somoza Ousted, 1979
Contra War, 1982 –1990
Sandinistas Defeated in Election, 1990

COSTA
RICA

PANAMA

CANAL
ZONE

Caracas

GRENADA

TRINIDAD and TOBAGO

VENEZUELA

GUYANA

Anti-U.S. Riots, 1959, 1964
Panama Canal Treaties, 1978
U.S. Invasion, 1989 –1990

Bogotá

COLOMBIA

SURINAME

FR. GUIANA

O.A.S. Charter, 1948
Drug War, 1989 –

Quito

ECUADOR

U.S.-backed Military
Coup, 1964
U.S.-supplied Fuel for
Nuclear Reactor, 1978
Rain Forest Crisis, 1990s

Tuna War with U.S., 1971

PERU

BRAZIL

PACIFIC OCEAN

Lima

BOLIVIA

Brasilia

Radical Military Junta to Power, 1968
Major Cocaine Source for U.S. Market, 1980s –1990s

La Paz

Che Guevara killed, 1967
Major Cocaine Source for
U.S. Market, 1980s –1990s

PARAGUAY

Rio de Janeiro

Asunción

Rio Pact Concluded,
1947

CHILE

U.S. Helped Oust
Allende, 1973

URUGUAY

Alliance for Progress
Launched, 1961

Santiago

Buenos Aires

Montevideo

ARGENTINA

Rule of Juan Perón,
1943 –1955, 1973 –1974

Pan-American Highway

U.S. Military sites

Soviet Missile sites, 1962

U.S. Direct Investments in Latin America:
1950 = $4.4 bil.   1970 = $11.1 bil.
1960 = $7.5 bil.   1980 = $38.7 bil.
1990 = $71.6 bil.

U.S. Foreign Aid (Grants and Credits):
1946 –1990 = $31.47 bil.

Argentine-British
War, 1982

FALKLAND IS.
(MALVINAS)

Map 2

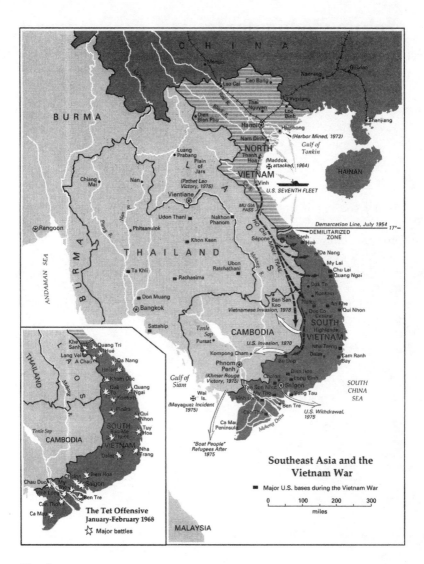

Map 3

Acknowledgements

Author and publishers are grateful to W.W. Norton & Company, Inc., New York, for permission to use Map 1 from *The American Age: U.S. Foreign Policy at Home and Abroad, Volume 2, since 1896*, second edition, by Walter Lafeber, also to Houghton Mifflin Company for permission to reproduce Map 2 and Map 3 from *American Foreign Relations: A History since 1895*, 4th edition, by Thomas G. Paterson, J. Garry Clifford and Kenneth J. Hagan, © 1995 by D.C. Heath and Company.

1   Introduction

The Cold War dominated international relations for over forty-five years (1945–1991). Within a framework of political relations, economic linkages, and military alliances, the Cold War was characterized by a high degree of tension between the United States and the Soviet Union; a costly and dangerous arms race; the polarization of domestic and international politics; the division of the world into economic spheres; and competition and conflict in the Third World. Understanding the Cold War is central to understanding the history of the second half of the twentieth century.

The Cold War shaped the foreign policies of the United States and the Soviet Union and deeply affected their societies and their political, economic, and military institutions. By providing a justification for the projection of US power and influence all over the world, the Cold War facilitated the assumption and assertion of global leadership by the United States. By providing Soviet dictator Joseph Stalin and his successors with an external enemy to justify their repressive internal regime, the Cold War helped legitimate an unrepresentative government and maintain the grip of the Communist Party on the Soviet Union.

In addition to its impact on the superpowers, the Cold War caused and perpetuated the division of Europe, and, within Europe, Germany. It also facilitated the reconstruction and reintegration of Germany, Italy, and Japan into the international system following their defeat in World War II. The Third World especially felt the effects of the Cold War, which overlapped with the era of decolonization and national liberation in the Third World. These two momentous processes had a profound and reciprocal effect on each other. The Cold War led to the division of Vietnam and Korea and to costly wars in both nations. Indeed, all but 200,000 of the more than 20 million people who died in wars between 1945 and 1990 were casualties in the more than one hundred wars that took place in the Third World in this period. In addition, most of the crises that threatened to escalate into nuclear war occurred in the Third World.

Far-reaching and long-lasting, the Cold War gave rise to a multitude of often conflicting interpretations regarding responsibility for its outbreak, its persistence, and its ultimate demise. Almost all of these interpretations were themselves shaped by the ongoing Cold War, and many were profoundly political in that the positions they argued were part of contemporary political as well as scholarly debates.

The end of the Cold War and the limited opening of archives in the former Soviet Union and its allies have not ended these debates. Nevertheless, the end of the Cold War provides an opportunity to move beyond fruitless, and often ahistorical, controversies over responsibility in order to understand what happened and why. It is now possible to ask new questions about the origins, persistence, and end of the Cold War.

To provide a fresh perspective, this study focuses on the interaction of international systemic factors and national politics and policies and looks at events all over the world. An international, as opposed to a national or binational, perspective is essential. Although Soviet–American rivalry was the dominant feature of the international system from 1945 to 1991, the Cold War encompassed much more than US–Soviet relations. It also involved political and economic competition among the core capitalist states, ideological conflict within and among states, and political, social, and economic change in the Third World. To understand the Cold War in all its dimensions, it is necessary to examine the interaction between changes in the global distribution of power; advances in weapons technology; shifts in the balances of social and political forces within and among nations; the evolution of the world economy; and the transformation of the Third World.

These various aspects of the Cold War were interrelated. The global distribution of power intersected with military technologies and strategies, ideological crosscurrents, the ongoing restructuring of economies and societies, and political, economic, and social change in the Third World to produce, prolong, and, eventually, end the Cold War. This study is organized chronologically in order to highlight the interaction of these factors.

In this book, emphasis is placed on structures and processes rather than individuals. I have chosen this focus not because individuals were unimportant but rather because it is essential to understand the larger contexts in which individuals acted. While an ideal history of the Cold War would include both, a study of this length cannot. For the same reasons, this study does not deal in depth with the domestic sources of foreign policy. Although domestic dynamics were very important, I have chosen to focus on the international dimensions of the Cold War.

I have tried to be balanced and fair, but I have given my own views on important issues. Due to the brevity of this book, I have not always found it possible to alert readers to alternative interpretations. I also regret that the format of this series does not allow me to provide detailed references to the many fine studies I have relied on in crafting this account of the Cold War. This is a work of synthesis, and while I alone am responsible for what I have written, I want to acknowledge my debt to others. In addition to the works cited in the Notes, I have tried to list the main works I found useful for this study in the Suggested Further Reading. I am also especially grateful to William Burr, Eric Evans, Benjamin Fordham, Robert McMahon, John McNeill, Aviel Roshwald, Richard Stites, Nancy Bernkopf Tucker, John Voll, and J. Samuel Walker, who took time from their own work to read and comment on a draft of this study. An early version of the approach utilized in this study appeared in my essay "Cold War" in the *Encyclopedia of U.S. Foreign Relations*. I want to thank Oxford University Press for permission to utilize portions of that essay, and Thomas G. Paterson for his help and advice on that project. I also want to express my appreciation to my editors at Routledge, especially Heather McCallum, for their assistance and patience.

I have endeavored to write a non-nationalist history. Although the relative emphasis on the United States and its actions is, in part, due to my personal background and professional training, it is also due to the dominant role the United States played in the Cold War.

This study is not the last word on the Cold War. Rather its purpose is to provide a reliable starting point from which interested readers can explore for themselves the conflict that dominated international relations in the second half of the twentieth century.

2 The Cold War begins, 1945–50

Following World War II, the foreign policies of the United States and the Soviet Union interacted with the chaotic and fluid state of international relations to produce the Cold War. Understanding the impact of World War II on the international system and its members is crucial to understanding the origins of the Cold War. World War II accelerated fundamental changes in the global distribution of power, in weapons technology, in the balance of political forces among and within nations, in the international economy, and in relations between the industrial nations and the Third World. In addition, the diplomatic and military decisions made during the war had a profound impact on the shape of the postwar world.

THE WORLD IN 1945

World War II was the culmination of a series of events that profoundly changed the global distribution of power. As National Security Council Paper No. 68, the seminal statement of US Cold War policies, pointed out in April 1950, "within the past thirty-five years the world has experienced two global wars of tremendous violence . . . two revolutions – the Russian and the Chinese – of extreme scope and intensity . . . the collapse of five empires – the Ottoman, the Austro-Hungarian, German, Italian, and Japanese – and the drastic decline of two major imperial systems, the British and the French." The result was the end of the European era and the rise to dominance of two continental-size superpowers, the United States and the Soviet Union.[1]

Before World War II there were six great powers: Great Britain, France, Germany, the Soviet Union, Japan, and the United States. The United States entered the postwar era in a uniquely powerful position, its relative standing greatly increased by its mobilization and war effort, its allies exhausted, and its rivals defeated. Around 410,000 US citizens lost their lives in the war, but US farms, factories, mines, and transportation networks escaped unscathed. Wartime mobilization and production lifted the United States out of the depression, and during the war the US economy almost doubled in size. In 1945, the United States controlled around half the world's manufacturing capacity, most of its food surpluses, and a large portion of its financial reserves. The United States also held the lead in a wide range of technologies essential to modern warfare. Possession of extensive domestic energy supplies and control over access to the vast oil reserves of Latin America and the Middle East further contributed to the US position of global dominance.

Despite a rapid demobilization that reduced the level of its armed forces from 12.1 million in 1945 to 1.7 million by mid-1947, the United States still possessed the world's mightiest military machine. The US Navy controlled the seas, US air power dominated the skies, and the United States alone possessed atomic weapons and the means to deliver them. In addition, the US role in the defeat of fascism and US espousal of such principles as the four freedoms (freedom of speech and worship, freedom from want and fear) had earned tremendous international prestige for the United States.

Although analysts began to speak of a bipolar world, divided between roughly equal superpowers, the Soviet Union was a distant second, its power largely concentrated along its borders in Eastern Europe, the Middle East, and northeast Asia. World War II devastated the Soviet Union. Late twentieth-century estimates of Soviet war-related deaths range from 20 to 27 million. Six of the Soviet Union's fifteen republics had been occupied, in whole or in part, by the Germans, and extensive destruction of crop land, farm animals, factories, mines, transportation networks, and housing stock disrupted the Soviet economy and left it barely one-quarter the size of the US's. Though impressive, Soviet military capacity lagged behind that of the United States. The Red Army had emerged as a formidable fighting force, but the Soviets lacked a long-range strategic air force, possessed meager air defenses, and, aside from a large submarine force, had an ineffective navy. Soviet military forces demobilized rapidly following the war, from around 11.3 million troops in mid-1945 to some 2.9 million by early 1948. Finally, until August 1949, the Soviets also lacked atomic weapons.

The positioning of a large part of Soviet military power in Eastern Europe posed a potential threat to Western European security. The devastation and defeat of Germany and Japan, powers that historically checked Russian power in Central Europe and northeast Asia respectively, improved the Soviets' relative position, at least in the short run.

Similarly, the decline of British power opened opportunities for the Soviets to improve their position along their southern border in the Middle East. On the other hand, the measure of security the Soviet Union had enjoyed as a result of divisions among its capitalist rivals was now lost. The defeat of Germany and Japan and the weakening of Great Britain and France raised the possibility that the capitalist powers might unite under US leadership. The proximity of the Soviet Union to the main European and Asian powers also increased the likelihood that they would look to the United States for help in balancing Soviet power.[2]

Great Britain, the third major power in 1945, occupied an important position in the postwar international system due to its empire, its military power, and its role in the international economy. The empire, including such Commonwealth countries as Canada, Australia, and New Zealand, enabled Britain to function as a world power. Spanning the globe, the Commonwealth crucially provided the network of bases that allowed Britain to project its power throughout most of the world. After the war, the British maintained a large military establishment, and in 1952 added atomic weapons to the traditional pillars of the Royal Navy and the Royal Air Force. Britain's economy was the strongest in Europe in 1945, and the pound sterling currency area played an important role in the international economy.[3]

On the other hand, six years of warfare had cost Britain around 400,000 lives, wiped out a quarter of its prewar wealth, and resulted in a massive external debt. Maintaining its military might severely strained Britain's precarious financial position. Moreover, the Commonwealth countries were essentially independent: India had been promised independence, Britain's other Asian colonies were restive, and Britain's influence in the Middle East was in decline.

The other prewar great powers were in even worse shape. Humiliated by its collapse in World War II, severely damaged by the Nazi occupation and the war, and deeply divided over the issue of collaboration, France was in danger of slipping from the ranks of the great powers. Around 600,000 Frenchmen had died in the war, and France also faced rising unrest in many parts of its empire that threatened to turn its once valuable colonies into liabilities. Its second bid for European hegemony thwarted, Germany had suffered severe damage during the war. Around 7 million Germans had died in the war, and Germany's cities were leveled, its transportation networks disrupted, and a large portion of its population displaced. Occupied by its enemies, Germany faced the prospect of partition. Around 3 million Japanese had died in the war, and Japan lay in ruins, devastated by the relentless US strategic bombing campaign that had culminated in the August 1945 atomic attacks on Hiroshima and Nagasaki. Shorn of its colonial empire, Japan was occupied by US forces.

Changes in the technology of war reinforced the shifts in the global balance of power. Conventional weapons had reached new heights of destructiveness during World War II. Power projection capabilities had taken a large leap forward as the long-range bomber and the aircraft carrier extended the reach of death and destruction. The systematic application of science to warfare resulted in new technologies – radar, the jet engine, cruise and ballistic missiles, and the atomic bomb – that opened new and terrifying prospects. The atomic bomb was especially frightening because it magnified the destructive force of warfare to a previously unimagined scale and concentrated that destruction in time.

The atomic bomb's potential to revolutionize warfare quickly made it an important focus of international relations. Some analysts, assuming rapid and widespread proliferation of atomic weapons, argued that the mere existence of such weapons would discourage aggression due to the near certainty of retaliation. Others, driven by fears of an "atomic Pearl Harbor," were convinced that heightened military preparedness and possibly even pre-emptive strikes were the best ways to safeguard national security in the atomic age. The appearance of weapons capable of such massive destruction started an arms race as the Soviet Union, Great Britain, and subsequently other nations sought to develop their own atomic weapons, and the United States sought to maintain its lead in atomic capability.

At the other end of the technological scale, the diffusion of military technology lessened the power gap between the industrial nations and the Third World. Equally important, Third World nationalist elites were able to organize peasants into formidable fighting forces that could hold their own against Western armies. This emergence of "lethal peasant armies" was particularly important in Asia, where the Chinese Communists had refined guerrilla tactics and had begun to master large-unit warfare.

Changes in the balance of political forces both within and among nations during and after World War II further complicated international relations. The potential impact of internal political alignments on the global balance of power invested domestic political struggles with international political and strategic significance.

Transnational ideological conflict had been especially important in the 1930s, with the Spanish Civil War providing the most notable example. The basic assumption was that a regime's internal ideological underpinnings would significantly influence, if not determine, its international alignment. Nations internally dominated by fascist or militarist

forces – Germany, Italy, and Japan – collaborated. The liberal democratic powers – Great Britain, France, and the United States – tended
to share similar interests though they often found it hard to work
together. The only communist great power, the Soviet Union, stood
alone, without allies until August 1939, when Stalin and Hitler signed a
non-aggression pact that cleared the way for their conquest and partition
of Poland the following month.

The German invasion of the Soviet Union in June 1941 ended the
Nazi–Soviet alliance and brought Great Britain, the Soviet Union, and
later the United States together in a grand alliance against Hitler. Subsequently, World War II, both internationally and within nations, largely
pitted the right – Germany, Italy, and Japan – against an uneasy alliance
of the center – Britain (along with its empire and Commonwealth) and
the United States – and the left – the Soviet Union. (France had surrendered to Germany in June 1940.) With the defeat of the right in the war,
the major fault line in international relations and within most nations
shifted to the left, reflecting and underpinning the emerging tension
between the United States and the Soviet Union.

By the end of World War II, the future of capitalism as an organizing principle for society was anything but secure. Already on the
defensive due to the depth and duration of the Great Depression,
capitalism and conservative parties in general also suffered in the eyes
of many from association with fascism. The struggle against fascism
had expanded to include opposition to authoritarianism and racism,
and the defeat of fascism in the international arena discredited the far
right in many nations.

The economic climate after the war tended to favor the political left.
The experiences of depression and global war accentuated existing
social, economic, and political divisions and generated popular
demands for widespread land, welfare, and economic reform. Wartime
controls had accustomed people to an increased government role in the
economy, and many people believed that economic planning would be
necessary to ensure economic growth and equity after the war. Among
the major capitalist powers, only the United States underwent a shift to
the right. Conservative opposition to the New Deal had continued to
gain strength during the war, and in the 1946 midterm elections the
Republicans captured control of both houses of Congress. While these
developments effectively contained further advances, they did not roll
back the main achievements of the New Deal – unionization of heavy
industry, Social Security, farm subsidies, and the beginning of civil
rights concerns. British politics, in contrast, moved to the left with the
victory of the Labour Party in July 1945, as deep-seated desires for

thoroughgoing social and economic reform outweighed gratitude to Prime Minister Winston Churchill for his wartime leadership.

The Soviet Union entered the postwar era with enhanced prestige because of the key role it played in defeating Nazi Germany. Within the Soviet Union the victory over Nazism solidified support, or at least tolerance, for continued communist rule and provided a sustaining myth for the communist regime. Unlike the Tsarist regime a generation earlier that had collapsed under the impact of World War I, the Soviet Union had, albeit at great cost, repelled the German invader and emerged victorious. Throughout Europe and in parts of the Third World communist parties and other leftist groups had gained ground as a result of their participation in resistance movements during the war and as a consequence of chaotic social, economic, and political conditions. In Eastern Europe, communists benefitted from the presence as well as the prestige of the Red Army. In countries such as France, Italy, Greece, China, and Vietnam, communists and their allies appeared poised to take power on their own. In Greece, only the introduction of over 30,000 British troops prevented communist-led resistance forces from taking power in late 1944. In addition, for many people in the Third World the Soviet Union seemed to offer a model for a rapid transition from a backward and weak agrarian society to a modern industrial power.

The chaotic state of the international economy was another important source of tension that threatened to rekindle conflict within and among nations. In the 1930s, the world had, in effect, split into relatively closed trading blocs. The United States had turned inward and, to a lesser extent, toward Latin America; Great Britain and other colonial powers had closed off their empires behind financial and trade barriers; Germany had built up an informal economic empire in central and southeastern Europe through a system of managed bilateral trade agreements; the Soviet Union had focused on building "socialism in one country" through collectivization of agriculture and forced industrialization; and Japan had attempted to extend its economic sway beyond the home islands and its colonial empire and organize East Asia in a self-sufficient co-prosperity sphere. A downward spiral of international trade and national production had ensued as attempts by individual countries to protect their economies and defend their shares of international trade at the expense of others elicited countermeasures which further restricted trade and production, deepened and prolonged the depression, and exacerbated international tensions.[4]

Wartime mobilization intensified the autarkic economic policies of the 1930s as the pressures of total war forced nations to harness economic processes to political and military purposes. The United States, Great Britain, and forty-two other countries had fashioned multilateral monetary arrangements and financial institutions at the Bretton Woods Conference in the summer of 1944. These envisioned a reformed and reconstructed international economy free from restrictive trade and financial barriers. Trade and financial controls, which had proliferated as part of the war effort, continued into the postwar period, however. The continuation of controls, coupled with the destruction and disruption caused by the war, seemed to some observers to foreshadow a repeat of the experience of the 1930s – economic stagnation, followed by political extremism and interstate conflict.

World War II also generated an anti-imperial thrust, and movements toward independence and national liberation in the Third World created significant tension in the postwar international system. Independence movements blossomed, especially throughout postwar Asia where the wartime spread of the Japanese empire had supplanted Western colonial regimes. The collapse of colonial authority encouraged the aspirations of local nationalists.

With defeat, Japan lost control of its colonies, Taiwan and Korea, and the client state it had established in Manchuria in 1931–32. Japanese expansion into China in the 1930s had partly interrupted the ongoing internal struggle for power between the Nationalists, led by Chiang Kai-shek, and the Communists, and had intensified Chinese efforts to regain control over their nation's destiny. Long-lasting and very destructive, World War II cost around 12 million Chinese their lives. After the defeat of Japan the civil war resumed as the Nationalists and Mao Zedong's Communists, who had grown in strength and popularity as a result of their resistance to the Japanese, fought for control of China. In Southeast Asia, the British, French, and Dutch faced nationalist challenges to their control of Malaya (Malaysia), Indochina (Vietnam, Laos, and Cambodia), and Indonesia respectively. In addition, the British faced well-organized and popular independence movements in India, Burma, and Ceylon (Sri Lanka).

The position of European colonial powers in the Middle East was less dramatically affected by the war. Nevertheless, challenges to French control – in Lebanon, Syria, Algeria, Tunisia, and Morocco – and to British influence – in Palestine, Egypt, and Iraq – threatened the Western position in the Middle East, fueled internal power struggles, and provided potential openings for the expansion of Soviet influence. British and Soviet troops had invaded Iran in 1941, replaced the pro-German shah with his twenty-one-year-old son, and occupied the strategically located country for the duration of the war. The United States had also become deeply involved in Iran, sending 30,000 troops to help operate the supply line from the Persian Gulf to the Soviet Union and several advisory missions to help the Iranian government cope with changed conditions. In addition to exacerbating great power rivalry for influence in Iran, the war experience disrupted the Iranian economy, causing widespread hardship and polarizing Iranian politics. Turkey remained technically neutral during the war, but the Turkish government had allowed German warships to enter the Black Sea through the Bosphorus, Sea of Marmara, and Dardanelles while denying Soviet warships similar privileges.

World War II in Africa was largely limited to the campaigns in North Africa so there was far less disruption of colonial rule than in Southeast Asia. Although Italy forfeited its colonies of Libya, Ethiopia (acquired in 1936), Somaliland, and Eritrea, the major colonial powers – Great Britain, France, Belgium, and Portugal – retained their colonies. The war stimulated economic development and brought social changes such as industrialization and urbanization that would soon have a political impact. In addition, the war against fascism had undermined racist justifications for colonial rule. (Ironically, wartime mobilization had strengthened the political power of white settlers in Kenya and parts of southern Africa.) Nationalist movements were not yet strong enough to challenge colonial authority, however, and uprisings against French rule in Madagascar were brutally suppressed.

Although most Latin American nations had won their independence in the nineteenth century, postwar Latin America was also ripe for change. Narrow openings for democratization arose in several countries during World War II as industrialization, urbanization, and wartime inflation spurred political mobilization. In addition, the fight against fascism created expectations of political and economic reform, and led to increased political participation by students and the middle class. Miners, factory workers, and some rural laborers also organized and became politically active, and communist parties expanded their memberships dramatically. Reformist parties won elections in several countries, and in Ecuador, Guatemala, El Salvador, Brazil, and Venezuela military or military-backed dictatorships fell to broad-based reformist movements. These developments deeply distressed the region's middle classes as well as entrenched traditional and military elites. They also raised concerns in the United States, which had significant economic interests in Latin America and a long-standing interest in political stability in the region.

Although the United States, Great Britain, and the Soviet Union were able to cooperate in defeating Germany and Japan, they were not able to overcome completely the distrust growing out of their prewar relations. The United States and Britain remembered that the Soviets had cooperated with Hitler between August 1939 and June 1941, and had not joined the war against Japan until it was almost over.[5] The United States also emphasized the large amount of lend-lease assistance, around $11 billion, that it had provided the Soviet Union.

The Soviets, for their part, had not forgotten Western hostility to their revolution and Western intervention in their civil war (1918–20), and they suspected that appeasement and Western refusal in the 1930s to cooperate against Hitler had been part of a plan to turn Hitler's attention to the east. The Soviets also emphasized that they had borne the brunt of the fighting against Hitler. US lend–lease aid made up less than 10 percent of total Soviet expenditures and did not arrive in quantity until after the battle of Stalingrad (August 1942–February 1943), which was the turning point in the war against Hitler. Most of all, the Soviets resented the Western Allies' delay in opening a second front in Europe. The delay meant that the Red Army had continued to do most of the fighting and dying until the summer of 1944, when Allied landings in Normandy finally diverted significant numbers of German troops from the Eastern Front.

The Soviets were aware that the United States, with British and Canadian assistance, had developed atomic weapons during the war and had withheld information about the bomb from them. Although their primary motive for using atomic bombs against Japan in August 1945 was to end the war quickly, US leaders also hoped that possession of atomic weapons would enhance their leverage in shaping the peace. Ending the war quickly not only saved lives; it limited Soviet gains in Asia and freed US forces for possible use elsewhere.[6]

The atomic bomb changed the strategic calculations of both sides. American possession of the bomb lessened the need for the Red Army to help control Germany and thus made the United States less willing to acquiesce in a Soviet sphere of influence in Eastern Europe or to accept Soviet advances in the Middle East and Asia. The bomb stiffened Soviet determination to control Eastern Europe because of the increased need to extend Soviet defenses against air attack. The US atomic monopoly also made the Soviets less willing to compromise on key issues lest they appear intimidated, and thus invite further pressure. Finally, US possession of atomic weapons increased Soviet determination to develop their own atomic arsenal.[7]

Nevertheless, during the war a common interest in defeating the Axis overshadowed difficulties and facilitated cooperation. The Yalta Conference, February 4–11, 1945, marked the high point in wartime cooperation among the allies. US President Franklin D. Roosevelt, British Prime Minister Winston Churchill, and Soviet leader Joseph Stalin agreed that they, joined by France, would occupy and control postwar Germany. The Soviets demanded that Germany pay heavy reparations to compensate its victims for the horrendous damage caused by Nazi aggression. (Heavy reparations would also weaken Germany and help rebuild Soviet strength.) The United States and Britain, how-ever, feared that heavy reparations would prevent economic recovery in Germany and throughout Europe. In the end, the three leaders agreed that Germany should pay reparations, but left the amount to be decided later. The Soviets had taken control of disputed territory in eastern Poland in 1939, and the three leaders agreed that Poland should be compensated by taking territory from Germany. Roosevelt and Churchill also agreed to accept the Soviet-supported provisional Polish government on the condition that it be enlarged by the inclusion of "democratic" elements and that it promise to hold free elections. In a Declaration on Liberated Europe, the three leaders pledged to help liberated nations solve their problems by democratic means. They also decided to extend the wartime alliance through the creation of a United Nations Organization. Finally, the Soviets agreed to enter the war against Japan within three months of the end of the war in Europe.

Although later criticized for ceding Eastern Europe to the Soviets, the Yalta agreements in fact reflected the existing balance of power. At the time of the conference, Soviet forces were in control of most of Eastern Europe and the eastern third of Germany. Western forces, in contrast, were still recovering from the December 1944 counterattack of Hitler's forces and had yet to cross the Rhine River. What historian Diane Shaver Clemens has called the spirit of Yalta – an atmosphere of con-ciliation and cooperation in which each nation gained what it sought most and made compromises on matters of vital interest to the others – was based, to a great extent, on mutual need. The West depended on the Red Army (primarily against Germany but also potentially against Japan), and the Soviet Union needed economic and military aid from the United States.[8]

By the time the leaders of the United States, Great Britain, and the Soviet Union met at the Potsdam Conference in July 1945, Germany had surrendered and postwar rivalry was fast replacing wartime cooper-ation. Nevertheless, the three allies reached final agreement on dividing Germany into four occupation zones (US, British, French, and Soviet), on Germany's boundaries, and on reparations. They also finalized plans for Soviet participation in the war against Japan. In the case of bound-aries, Germany forfeited its conquests and lost some territory to Poland

and the Soviet Union. The three leaders – Harry S. Truman, who had succeeded Roosevelt in April; Clement Attlee, who replaced Churchill during the conference; and Stalin – decided that the main source of reparations for each power would be its own occupation zone, with limited provisions for some Soviet access to resources from the Western zones, which covered the more industrialized parts of Germany.

THE STRUGGLE FOR EUROPE

The end of the war removed the main incentive for cooperation and made all three less inclined to compromise. US and British willingness to respect the Soviet Union's vital interests ended with Germany's defeat and the successful test of the atomic bomb, which greatly lessened their need for Soviet help. Similarly, the defeat of Germany and Japan lessened Soviet willingness to defer to Western interests and sensitivities.

Despite the lingering presence of isolationist sentiment in parts of the United States, the experience of World War II facilitated broad public acceptance of a global conception of US national security interests and requirements. Drawing on what they believed to be the lessons of the 1930s, US leaders sought to create and maintain a favorable balance of power in Europe and Asia, to fashion an international economic environment open to US trade and investment, and to maintain the integration of the Third World in the world economy in an era of decolonization and national liberation. To achieve these goals, US leaders believed that the United States had to have an overseas base system that would provide the nation with defense in depth and allow it to deter aggression by projecting power into potential trouble spots. US leaders also believed that the United States should maintain its monopoly of atomic weapons in order to deter, and if necessary punish, potential aggressors. US security policies were designed not only to protect the physical security of the United States and its allies but to preserve a broadly defined "American way of life" by constructing an international order that would be open to and compatible with US interests and ideals.[9]

President Roosevelt had hoped to achieve these goals in cooperation with the Soviet Union, though with the Soviets playing a subordinate, regional role. Roosevelt died in April 1945, however, and hopes for peaceful coexistence died with him. His successor, Harry S. Truman, faced a changed international environment. The political vacuum created by the collapse of German and Japanese power and the changed balance of political forces in the rest of Europe and Asia seemed to offer the Soviet Union and its ideological allies plentiful opportunities to expand their power and influence. Expansion of Soviet power and influence threatened to complicate, if not prevent, the implementation of US plans for the postwar world.

World War II also profoundly affected Soviet security perceptions and policies. Before the early 1990s, the almost total lack of availability of primary sources on Soviet foreign policy made it extremely difficult to discern Soviet motives with any degree of certainty. Despite the opening of a large number of records to researchers, the amount of primary material on Soviet foreign policies in these years is still fairly limited. Although scholars now know far more about Soviet foreign policy than previously, they remain divided over many key issues. In particular, the influence of the Stalinist system on the objectives, as distinct from the means, of Soviet foreign policy has remained a hotly contested issue. Many scholars still see Stalin as an incorrigible ideologue and expansionist. In contrast, others have questioned the long-assumed links between Stalin's repressive internal regime and Soviet foreign policy, and have reassessed the impact of Marxism–Leninism and totalitarianism on Soviet foreign policy. They highlight Russian history and geography, bureaucratic differences within the Soviet decision-making elite, and the security requirements arising from the Soviet Union's unique geopolitical position.[10]

Soviet security objectives at the end of World War II included creating strong safeguards against future German aggression, secure borders, and a buffer zone in Eastern Europe; reconstructing the Soviet Union's war-damaged industrial base; and maintaining a strong military, including the development of atomic weapons. The Soviets initially sought cooperation with the United States to achieve these goals. The United States was the only nation that could provide the large-scale economic assistance the Soviets desired, as well as being the only country with the power to prevent the Soviet Union from attaining its other objectives. Regardless of possible hopes for postwar cooperation with the United States, the Soviet Union's key objectives – circumscribing German power and maintaining a secure sphere of influence in Eastern Europe – ran up against Western ideals, economic objectives, and security requirements.

Soviet leaders were painfully aware that their country possessed an economic base vastly inferior to that of the United States. To close the gap, the Soviets desperately desired extensive reparations from Germany to rebuild their economy and to reduce Germany's military potential. The Western powers controlled the bulk of Germany's industrial assets, however, and the Soviet goal of limiting German power clashed with US plans to promote German and European economic recovery. US and other Western officials also suspected that the Soviets opposed economic recovery in Germany and Europe in hopes that poor economic conditions would enhance the political prospects of communist parties.

Without extensive reparations from Germany or aid from the United States, the other options for obtaining resources for reconstruction were to exact resources from Eastern Europe and/or from the Soviet people. Both options contained significant drawbacks. Eastern Europe and the Soviet Union were poorer than Germany and both had also suffered extensive damage during the war. Exacting resources from the Soviet people meant the reimposition of harsh economic and political controls. Exacting resources from Eastern Europe deprived the peoples of the region of the resources they needed for reconstruction and development and clearly clashed with Soviet efforts to build a secure sphere of influence in Eastern Europe. After 1946, however, these were the only options left.[11] The Western allies refused to permit extensive reparations from their zones in Germany, and it had become clear that the United States would not provide aid without imposing unacceptable political conditions. As he had in the late 1920 and 1930s, Stalin responded by instituting a harsh program of economic reconstruction that imposed heavy burdens on workers and peasants and sacrificed consumption to investment in heavy industry. He also clamped down on dissent.

The Soviets also turned to Eastern Europe. Between 1945 and 1955, the Soviets extracted an estimated $13 billion worth of resources from Eastern Europe and their occupation zone in Germany. Although these resources were crucial to the rebuilding of the Soviet economy and Soviet military power, the economic extractions, coupled with repressive political practices, irreparably damaged Soviet relations with Eastern Europe.

By the end of the war the Soviets had reabsorbed Estonia, Latvia, and Lithuania and annexed small portions of Czechoslovakia, Romania, and Germany. In short order they also installed subservient regimes in Poland, Romania, Bulgaria, and their occupation zone in Germany. In addition, local communist parties had gained positions of influence in Czechoslovakia and Hungary, and dominated Yugoslavia and Albania.

The establishment of communist regimes in Eastern Europe was not solely the result of a conscious effort by the Soviet Union to dominate the region. World War II had created revolutionary conditions in

Eastern Europe by disrupting social, political, and economic structures. Under German pressure, the prewar governments had collaborated with the Nazis or collapsed and gone into exile, leaving a vacuum of authority at war's end into which communists and other groups moved.

In addition to the annihilation of the region's Jews, the mass exodus of ethnic Germans before the advancing Red Army and the expulsion of Germans by postwar regimes disrupted the region's economic life. Germans had made up an important part of Eastern Europe's property-owning classes and had expanded their holdings during the war by taking over property owned by Jews and other "enemies" of the Third Reich. These properties passed into the hands of the newly formed postwar governments, thus facilitating land reform and the nationalization of banking and industry.

Soviet efforts to create more secure borders by means of supporting cooperative governments in neighboring countries not only ran up against Soviet reconstruction requirements but were complicated by hostile local populations that the Soviets often harshly repressed. Soviet use of such means as fraudulent elections, a controlled press, and suppression of dissent to maintain their influence in Eastern Europe also exacerbated tensions with the West, which viewed Soviet actions in Eastern Europe as an indicator of overall Soviet intentions. To many observers, Stalin seemed to believe that only countries controlled by communist parties could be trusted to respect the Soviet Union's security needs.

The expansion of Soviet power and influence into central and Eastern Europe alarmed US and Western leaders. The United States and its European allies feared that Soviet domination of Eastern Europe could limit access to needed markets, foodstuffs, and raw materials, as well as pose a security threat to Western Europe. Drawing on an influential February 1946 analysis – the "long telegram," by George F. Kennan, a young State Department Soviet specialist serving in Moscow – US leaders began to view the Soviet Union as an intractable foe and to fashion a foreign policy that focused on containing the spread of Soviet power and communist influence.

US leaders were aware that the Soviet Union was too weak to risk a war. Confident in the military power of the United States, they did not expect the Soviets to attack Western Europe or other vital areas. Rather they feared that communists and other groups sympathetic to the Soviet Union and hostile to capitalism and the West could exploit postwar vacuums of power in Germany and Japan, socio-economic dislocation in Europe, civil war in China and Greece, and decolonization and nationalism in the Third World to take power. US policymakers assumed that regardless of where and how communist parties gained control, they would pursue policies that served Soviet interests. Such gains could turn the global balance of power against the United States, deny US companies and the US economy access to important markets, raw materials, and investment opportunities, and eventually jeopardize economic and political freedom in the United States.

To avoid such outcomes, US policymakers believed that they had to find a way to rebuild the world economy, beginning with the reconstruction of Western Europe and Japan. Economic growth would prevent another depression and help mitigate class conflict, thus weakening the appeal of leftist groups. Air power and atomic weapons could provide the shield behind which these measures could be implemented without provoking a pre-emptive attack by the Soviet Union.

Soviet actions in the year following the war seemed to confirm the accuracy of Kennan's concerns. The Soviets rejected the US plan for the international control of atomic energy, presented to the United Nations in the summer of 1946 by Bernard Baruch. They charged that the plan's provisions, which allowed the United States to retain its atomic arsenal until an international control system was fully functioning to US satisfaction, preserved the US atomic monopoly while preventing other nations from developing atomic weapons. The Soviets also objected to the Baruch Plan's demand that the permanent members of the UN Security Council give up their right of veto in matters relating to atomic energy. The United States was unwilling to change the key provisions of its plan, and the Soviets blocked its adoption by the United Nations Security Council in December 1946.

Declining British power, regional rivalries, and internal political polarization combined in Iran, Greece, and Turkey to fuel Cold War tensions. In early 1946, the Soviets delayed withdrawing their occupation forces from northern Iran, as agreed in a 1942 treaty with that country, while supporting separatist movements in Azerbaijan and Kurdistan and demanding oil rights covering Iran's northern provinces. Even after Iran, with strong US support, had taken the matter to the United Nations, the Soviets did not withdraw their forces until Iran agreed to allow Soviet participation in oil development in northern Iran and a peaceful resolution of the separatist issue. At the same time, the civil war in Greece resumed when communist-led guerrillas took up arms against the corrupt, repressive, and unrepresentative Greek government after disputed elections and the continuation of government-sponsored right-wing terrorism. Although Soviet involvement in Greece was minimal, the Yugoslav communists provided aid to the Greek rebels. In addition, the Soviets renewed pressure on Turkey to revise the terms of the agreement governing access to the Black Sea and to grant them base rights along the straits between the Black Sea and the Mediterranean.

The Truman Doctrine of March 1947 called for the global containment of communism and elicited the political support that enabled US leaders to act on their beliefs about the relationship between politics, economics, and US security. New government institutions reinforced the shift to a more activist foreign policy. The National Security Act of 1947 established the National Security Council to advise the president on foreign affairs and defense policy; created the Central Intelligence Agency to gather and analyze foreign intelligence and conduct covert operations; and created a Department of Defense to coordinate the activities of the branches of the US armed forces.

Anti-communism provided a framework for understanding a complicated world and resonated with traditions that ran deep in US society and political culture. US leaders regarded communism as a strategic threat because of its connections with Soviet power, and as an ideological and economic threat because of its hostility to private property and free markets, concepts that many Americans linked directly to political freedom. In addition to its more conservative variants, an anti-communist liberalism re-emerged that focused on communism's denial of political and civil rights rather than its limits on economic freedom. Anti-communism became a guiding principle of US foreign policy and a significant force in US domestic politics. It provided an explanation for what was wrong in the world; a prescription for what to do about it; and an ideological justification for US actions.

In addition to calling for the global containment of communism, Truman specifically requested military and economic aid for Greece and Turkey. US aid to the former eliminated the Greek government's incentive to enact reforms to gain popular support. Instead, the government pursued a military solution to the civil war. Stalin remained unwilling to provide meaningful assistance to the Greek communists, and after the rift between the Soviet Union and Yugoslavia (see below), the Yugoslavs halted their aid to the Greek communists, who unwisely sided with Stalin. US assistance to Turkey not only bolstered Turkey's determination to resist Soviet pressure, but provided the United States with forward bases to support aerial assaults on the Soviet Union in the event of war.

US actions in Greece, Turkey, and Iran demonstrated determination to resist communism and to maintain Western access to Middle East oil. Both were linked to the core US concern about economic and political conditions in Western Europe. Although economic conditions improved in most of Western Europe in 1946, recovery faltered in 1947, due to a fuel crisis resulting from the unusually harsh winter of 1946–47, social unrest, political instability, and declining foreign exchange reserves. In the case of Germany, where there was little economic recovery, the problems were the political impasse among the occupying powers and French and Soviet determination to exact reparations from their occupation zones regardless of the consequences.

Although wartime destruction was extensive, Western Europe's economic difficulties had more to do with trade and payments problems than with physical destruction. World War II had shattered Europe's prewar trade and payments patterns. Within Europe, the collapse of German production was the key problem because without German coal and manufactured exports, other European countries were forced to turn to the United States for their needs. In addition, widespread destruction in Eastern Europe, and its political isolation from the West, cut off an important non-dollar source of food and raw materials and an important market for manufactured goods. Forced to turn to the United States for food, fuel, and manufactured goods, especially capital equipment, the countries of Western Europe faced a dollar shortage – they needed imports from the United States, but they were unable to earn the dollars necessary to pay for their needs.

Before the war, Europe had obtained the dollars to pay for imports from the United States through earnings on foreign investments, shipping and insurance services, sales of colonial raw materials to the United States, and US investment in Europe and its colonies. To finance the war effort Britain and other Western European countries had liquidated much of their foreign investment, and shipping earnings fell due to wartime losses at sea. Colonial earnings fell due to independence movements in key dollar-earning colonies and declining terms of trade for key commodities. In addition, US investors after the war concentrated on the booming US domestic market and investment opportunities in Middle East and Venezuelan oil rather than running the risks of political instability in Europe.

US leaders feared that economic distress would translate into support for communist parties, especially in France and Italy. At the least, Western European countries might expand economic controls that limited trade and investment or be tempted to make trade arrangements with the Soviet Union that would provide the Soviets with added influence in Western Europe. To solve these problems, the United States, following Secretary of State George C. Marshall's June 1947 call for a European recovery program, provided Western Europe with billions of dollars in economic assistance.[12] Most of this assistance (90 percent in the case of Marshall Plan aid) was in the form of grants, which helped Western

Europe avoid debts that could impede recovery. This assistance paid for vital imports, allowing the participating countries to obtain the raw materials, fuel, and foodstuffs they needed for reconstruction.

Marshall Plan aid had political as well as economic consequences. US assistance allowed centrist governments to devote massive resources to reconstruction and to expand their countries' exports without imposing politically unacceptable and socially divisive austerity programs that would have been necessary without US aid. Although allowing creation of the modern European welfare state, US aid helped counteract what US leaders saw as a dangerous drift away from free enterprise and toward collectivism. By favoring some policies and opposing others the United States not only influenced how Western European elites defined their own interests but altered the internal balance of power among the decision-making groups. In addition, covert-action programs undermined communist influence in trade unions and other institutions. The overall impact of US aid policies was to narrow the scope of acceptable debate and facilitate the ascendancy of centrist parties such as the Christian Democrats in West Germany and Italy.

US support for European-wide planning and such institutions as the European Payments Union helped promote European economic integration. In addition to the Economic Cooperation Administration established to manage US foreign-assistance programs, the United States encouraged Western European governments, joined by the military governors of the Western zones in Germany, to set up the Organization for European Economic Cooperation to coordinate aid requests. US leaders supported European integration because they believed that creation of a larger economic unit would encourage economies of scale, spark technical innovation, and increase productivity. A more productive Europe would be able to overcome the dollar gap without exchange and trade controls and would contribute to an open and prosperous world economy. A more prosperous Europe would also erode the appeal of communist parties and ensure that Western Europe remained capitalist and aligned with the United States.

Rebuilding German economic strength was crucial to the recovery of the European economy. German reconstruction offered a solution to the problems of increasing European production and reducing Europe's dollar imports. The United States made Germany eligible for Marshall Plan aid and led the way in uniting the three Western occupation zones and moving them toward self-government.[13] To assuage Western European anxieties over the revival of German power and the danger of pre-emptive moves by the Soviet Union, the United States, Great Britain, and ten other nations forged the North Atlantic Treaty in

April 1949, which pledged its members to the common defense of Western Europe.

The Marshall Plan also solidified the division of Europe. Until mid-1947, the Soviets had pursued a relatively cautious policy in Europe that differed from country to country according to local circumstances. In contrast to their efforts to set up compliant governments in Poland, Romania, Bulgaria, and their zone in Germany, the Soviets had allowed relatively free elections in Hungary and Czechoslovakia in 1945, and had cooperated in the creation of representative governments in Austria and Finland. Even where communists controlled the government, the Soviets allowed "national communists" (communists who tried to adapt to local conditions rather than impose the Soviet model on their country) to lead. In addition, the Soviets had discouraged communist parties from taking revolutionary action in France, Italy, Greece, and Spain, and had urged the Yugoslav communists to limit their demands for territory and to cut back their support of the Greek guerrillas.

The US offer to include Eastern Europe in the Marshall Plan worried the Soviets. Fearing that Western aid would undermine their influence in the region, the Soviets prohibited Eastern European countries from participating in the Marshall Plan and created a new international communist organization, the Communist Information Bureau, known as Cominform. In addition, they concluded a series of trade agreements with Eastern Europe known as the Molotov Plan (superseded by the Council for Mutual Economic Assistance – Comecon – in 1949). They also supported successful efforts by local communists to end the "democratic interludes" in Hungary (1945–47) and Czechoslovakia (1945–48), and to begin the "Stalinization" of their societies by instituting collectivization of agriculture, adopting economic plans that favored heavy industry over consumption, and cracking down on dissent. Finally, the Soviets urged Western European communist parties to oppose the Marshall Plan.

Soviet efforts to force ideological and political uniformity in Eastern Europe led to a sharp split between the Soviet Union and Yugoslavia in 1948. Yugoslav communists led by Josip Broz Tito insisted on their right to determine their own domestic and foreign policies. The Tito–Stalin split further intensified Soviet efforts to control the internal affairs of the region and led to a series of purge trials throughout the region in 1948–52 that removed "national communists" from positions of authority and cut Eastern European communist parties off from their mass base, undermining what legitimacy they had earned during the war and in the immediate postwar years. While the short-term result was greater Soviet control over Eastern Europe, the long-term impact was counterproductive. Lacking indigenous sources of support, the communist regimes of Eastern Europe became a permanent source of tension and instability, and eventually a drain on Soviet resources.

Moreover, in a classic example of what international relations scholars call the "security dilemma" – the tendency for a country's quest for increased security to raise the anxieties of its prospective adversaries and to provoke countermeasures – Soviet attempts to force the West to take Soviet interests into account backfired and reinforced Western resolve to rebuild and defend western Germany and Western Europe. Although communist parties seized power in Hungary and Czechoslovakia, efforts by Western European communists to disrupt the Marshall Plan failed miserably and undermined popular support for those parties. Both actions increased Western suspicions of Soviet intentions. The Soviet imposition of a blockade on all land and water routes to Berlin (June 1948–May 1949) to protest against Western plans to unify and rebuild the three Western zones of Germany instead led to a Western airlift that won over German public opinion and helped pave the way for the creation of the Federal Republic of Germany in September 1949. The Soviets were forced to end their blockade of Berlin and to establish their own German state, the German Democratic Republic, in their occupation zone the following month. Similarly, Soviet efforts beginning in 1948 to strengthen and modernize their armed forces and their successful test of an atomic bomb in August 1949 raised Western suspicions and galvanized public support for Western efforts to maintain military superiority.

GLOBALIZING THE COLD WAR

The Marshall Plan and efforts to promote Japanese reconstruction (see below) also influenced Western policies toward the Third World, eventually pitting the United States and its allies against the rising tide of decolonization and revolutionary nationalism. US leaders believed that controlling access to the resources, markets, and labor of the Third World was crucial to containing the Soviet Union, to maintaining US leadership of the Western alliance, and to the economic health of the United States, Western Europe, and Japan. In particular, US leaders believed that expanding trade and investment in the Third World provided a way to overcome the dollar shortage. US investment and imports of raw materials would increase the flow of dollars to the Third World. Western Europe and Japan, in turn, could obtain the dollars they needed from the Third World through trade, taxation, and other means.

These dollars would allow Western Europe and Japan to purchase needed US inputs, thus promoting their reconstruction and supporting prosperity in the United States. Before and during World War II, the United States had opposed European colonialism for political and economic reasons, and resented the tendency of colonial powers to exclude US companies from their colonies. Politically, the United States believed that continued colonialism created instability and radicalized independence movements. After the war, however, the United States gradually began to view decolonization rather than its denial as leading to instability and creating conditions in which groups friendly to the Soviet Union and hostile to Western capitalism could take power. While still favoring independence as an ultimate goal, the United States began working more closely with colonial powers to ensure that successor governments were controlled by pro-Western elements.[14]

The Cold War also reinforced the traditional US determination to maintain an economic and strategic sphere of influence in Latin America. US anti-communism combined with local elite hostility to political and economic reform and with international economic pressures to close the window of opportunity for reform created by World War II. In a pattern common throughout the region, conservative groups and their military allies replaced reformist governments, banned communist parties, and repressed labor unions and peasant organizations.

Latin America's return to the right was closely related to the development strategy encouraged by the United States. In contrast to Western Europe, where Marshall Plan aid allowed reform and recovery to proceed in tandem, the United States refused Latin American requests for economic assistance and looked to the military and traditional elites to maintain a favorable climate for foreign investment. To secure its influence in Latin America further, the United States sponsored a regional security pact in 1947 (the Rio Treaty) and the formation of the Organization of American States in 1948. Latin American countries stressed the non-intervention principles enshrined in both organizations' charters. In contrast, the United States argued that the charters permitted collective intervention to protect the Americas from external threats and internal subversion.

Although Africa was distant from the main centers of Cold War conflict, the outbreak of the Cold War had an important impact on African developments. In southern Africa, the United States sought to exclude Soviet and leftist influence by supporting the colonial powers, Britain, France, Belgium, and Portugal, and the white minority government of the Union of South Africa. These governments were US allies in the struggle against communism, and southern Africa was rich in strategic minerals, including uranium, the key raw material needed to build atomic bombs. The United States strongly criticized the policy of apartheid instituted by the Nationalist Party after it took control of South Africa in 1948. Nevertheless, concerned about maintaining access to South Africa's resources, the United States soon forged a close security relationship with the fiercely anti-communist Nationalists.

World War II had demonstrated the crucial importance of oil to modern warfare, and after the war the United States looked to Middle Eastern oil to fuel European and Japanese economic recovery. Following the war, France was forced to grant independence to Lebanon and Syria (1946) and faced ultimately successful challenges to its control in Morocco, Tunisia, and Algeria. Weakened by the loss of the Indian Army, its main power projection force east of Suez, Britain's "moment" in the Middle East was beginning to end. The British withdrew from Palestine in 1948, leaving the United Nations to deal with the fighting that had already broken out between Arabs and Jews. The British also faced an increasingly powerful challenge to their privileged position in Egypt, where they controlled a huge military base complex in the Suez Canal zone as well as the Suez Canal Company. The British position in Iran, where the British-owned Anglo-Iranian Oil Company monopolized reserves and production and operated the largest refinery in the world at Abadan, was also becoming increasingly tenuous. Postwar Iran was very unstable as a result of the economic impact of the wartime occupation coupled with political struggle between the shah and the Majlis (parliament). In addition, competition among the Soviet Union, Great Britain, and the United States for oil and influence continued, and exacerbated Iran's growing political polarization as each supported different participants in the internal struggle for power.

US interest in postwar Asia centered on Japan and its former empire. Japan was the only industrial power in Asia and its wartime expansion had disrupted the balance of power in East Asia. Japanese expansion had altered the course of the Chinese revolution and undermined Western colonial rule in Southeast Asia, and Japan's defeat led to the independence of Korea and the return of Taiwan to China. The United States had played the major role in Japan's defeat and excluded its allies from the postwar occupation of the country. The United States initially planned to remake Japanese society, purging those elements responsible for the war and promoting democratization, demilitarization, and deconcentration of economic power. Early US-sponsored reforms included extending the suffrage, reforming land tenure, breaking up the *zaibatsu* (financial and industrial conglomerates), extending labor rights, and abolishing the military.

As relations with the Soviet Union deteriorated and civil war in China ruled out reliance on that country as a regional ally, the United States "reversed course" in 1947–48 and began emphasizing economic reconstruction and political stability in Japan. This change in focus halted reform and led to the rehabilitation of old elites and institutions believed to be necessary to re-establish political order and rebuild the economy. The United States did not rebuild the Japanese military, however. Japan had no neighbors strong enough to balance its strength; it did not face a security threat comparable to that facing Western Europe; and its citizens responded favorably to the demilitarization forced on them by the US-imposed 1947 constitution. As in the case of Germany, control of atomic weapons and over access to oil supplies allowed the United States to oversee economic reconstruction in a former enemy while at the same time preventing a revival of Japanese aggression. A rebuilt, industrial Japan would require access to food and raw materials and to markets for its products. Japan had traditionally looked to East Asia for raw materials and markets, but postwar Asia, like much of the Third World, was in turmoil.

Revolutions in the Third World often combined a national struggle against foreign domination with an internal social revolution. This combination was especially strong in postwar Asia. In the Philippines, however, these two aspects were separated when the United States redeemed its wartime pledge by granting the Philippines independence in 1946 (though it retained extensive military and economic privileges). Thus when electoral fraud and the resistance of the Filipino elite to land reform led to a rural rebellion led by elements of the wartime resistance movement, the Philippine government, with US economic and military assistance, was able to defeat the insurgency. Similarly, the British were able to defeat a communist-led insurgency supported by ethnic Chinese in Malaya through a combination of military measures and promises of independence. (In spite of US and British military assistance, it took until the mid-1950s to defeat the insurgents in both cases.) In South Asia, faced with well-organized and popular, but non-communist, independence movements, the British acted before the independence movements developed revolutionary aspirations. In addition, the cost of maintaining control had begun to exceed the benefits. The British granted independence to India–Pakistan in 1947, Ceylon (Sri Lanka) in 1947, and Burma in 1948.

The French and the Dutch, however, opposed independence movements with force. Indonesia and Indochina (along with Malaya) were important potential sources of Third World dollars for their colonial overlords, The Netherlands and France, respectively. In addition, both (along with the rest of Southeast Asia) could be important sources of raw materials for a rebuilding Japan, and markets for its products. Both experienced anti-colonial revolts in the late 1940s. In Vietnam, the communists, led by Ho Chi Minh, the best-known and most widely supported Vietnamese nationalist leader, dominated the independence movement. In contrast, despite a strong communist presence, non-communist nationalists constituted the leading force in the struggle for Indonesia's independence.

Although Soviet involvement was minimal, Cold War concerns deeply influenced the different outcomes. In Indonesia, the United States pressured the Dutch to turn power over to the non-communist nationalists rather than risk radicalization of the independence movement. In Vietnam, faced with the choice between an independence movement led by communists or the continuation of French colonial rule, the United States tried to find a third way by indirectly supporting the French war effort while urging the French to find and support non-communist Vietnamese nationalists. In both cases, US policymakers saw successful resolution of these conflicts as essential to achieving their economic, political, and military goals in Europe as well as in Asia.

Communists and other radical groups were also active throughout Korea, as the peninsula was rocked by widespread violence following the end of Japanese colonial rule. In the area north of the thirty-eighth parallel, Soviet occupation forces helped communist guerrilla leader Kim Il Sung eliminate his rivals and inaugurate a personal rule that lasted until his death in 1994. South of the dividing line, US occupation forces helped conservative Koreans led by Syngman Rhee defeat their moderate and leftist opponents and establish, under UN auspices, the Republic of Korea in September 1948. In response, Kim and his comrades proclaimed the formation of the Democratic People's Republic of Korea. Both regimes claimed jurisdiction over all of Korea, and border skirmishes and raids were common. Korea stood on the brink of civil war when Soviet occupation forces withdrew from North Korea in December 1948, followed by the exit of US occupation forces from South Korea six months later.

In China, the Communists, led by Mao Zedong and Zhou Enlai, triumphed in the civil war despite over $3 billion in US assistance to the Nationalists. The Communists proclaimed the establishment of the People's Republic of China (PRC) in October 1949. The Chinese model of revolutionary struggle based on the peasantry resonated throughout the Third World, and had a profound impact on the Cold War, even before Mao definitively turned to look to the Soviet Union for assistance.

Although the Soviets had given the Communists very little assistance and a great deal of bad advice, and had maintained relations with Chiang Kai-shek's regime almost to the end, the Soviets and the Communists, in early 1950, signed a security and economic assistance treaty.

Meanwhile, Chiang and 2 million of his supporters had retreated to the island of Taiwan, their days apparently numbered as the United States reconsidered its policy of support. In addition to Taiwan, the Nationalists kept control of several small island groups, including Jinmen (Quemoy) and Mazu (Matsu) just off the coast of Fujian Province. Chiang's government on Taiwan presented the United States with a dilemma. On the one hand, supporting Chiang or some other anti-communist leader would constitute interference in the Chinese revolution and earn the enmity of the People's Republic. On the other hand, many US strategists regarded Taiwan as an "unsinkable aircraft carrier," astride important shipping lanes and air routes and in a location that allowed the United States to project its power deep into the Asian mainland.

The Communist victory in China came at a time when economic recovery seemed to falter in Western Europe and Japan, and the United States experienced its first postwar economic downturn. In addition, the Soviet Union successfully tested an atomic bomb in August 1949. Faced with the loss of their atomic monopoly and continued instability in the Third World when limited resources were increasingly needed for European and Japanese recovery, US leaders feared that without corrective measures the global distribution of power could turn against the "free world."

To counter the Soviet atomic bomb, President Truman approved plans to manufacture more atomic weapons and decided to accelerate US development of a hydrogen bomb. He also approved a study of overall US force requirements. The result was a seminal document, NSC-68, drafted in early 1950 by State Department official Paul Nitze in close consultation with Secretary of State Dean Acheson. NSC-68 painted the Soviet Union as a relentlessly expansionist adversary that would exploit any and all opportunities to take over the world. Only US military superiority, they believed, had prevented the Soviets from trying to expand beyond the areas they controlled as a result of World War II. Now, with its atomic monopoly gone, the United States and its allies faced the prospect of renewed communist offensives. To prevent this from happening, NSC-68 called for the United States to undertake a "rapid build-up of the political, economic, and military strength" of the "free world."

Implementing NSC-68 would require a tripling of US military expenditures. Although Truman and his top defense and foreign policy advisers agreed with its recommendations, it was not clear that Congress could be convinced to come up with the money. The US political climate, and the Cold War, changed on June 25, 1950, however, when North Korean forces invaded South Korea.[15]

Recent research has revealed that in April 1950, Stalin, after rejecting previous pleas by North Korean leader Kim Il Sung for Soviet approval and assistance in taking over the South, agreed to supply the necessary military assistance. Stalin, however, conditioned his acquiescence on Kim's gaining the approval of China. It is still not clear why Stalin reversed his previous policy. The combination of the Communist victory in the Chinese civil war, the Soviet atomic bomb test, and Western economic difficulties might have convinced Stalin (and Mao, who agreed to Kim's plan) that the global balance of forces was moving in their favor. On the other hand, Stalin and Mao may have been worried about a resurgent Japan and the prospect of a US military build-up, and believed that they needed to gain control of South Korea to secure their position in Northeast Asia. A communist-controlled Korea would expand the buffer zone on Soviet borders, improve the Soviet strategic situation *vis-à-vis* rebuilding Japan, maintain Soviet leadership of the Asian revolution, and divert US attention from Europe.[16]

US leaders interpreted the North Korean attack in global terms as a test of Western resolve to resist communist aggression, and feared that failure to respond would undermine the credibility of US commitments and encourage neutralism. Determined to stand firm, the Truman administration secured a mandate from the United Nations to send US armed forces to aid the beleaguered South Koreans who were reeling in retreat from the Northern onslaught. The United Nations was able to act because the Soviet representative on the Security Council was boycotting the meeting in protest of the UN refusal to recognize the People's Republic of China as the rightful holder of China's place on the Security Council.

Surprised by the US reaction, the Soviets, who had provided not only military equipment but operational plans and some air support, carefully avoided large-scale and overt involvement in the war. The PRC, on the other hand, decided to intervene in the fall of 1950 after UN forces, commanded by US General Douglas MacArthur, ignored warnings not to approach the PRC's border with North Korea. Moreover, Mao apparently also wanted to use the war to mobilize public support for accelerating his own revolution and to deter US interference in China by punishing "American arrogance."

After heavy fighting the battle lines stabilized in the spring of 1951. When an armistice was finally arranged in July 1953, the dividing line between the two Koreas remained at the thirty-eighth parallel. Before it ended, the Korean War cost over 3 million people their lives, including over 50,000 US servicemen and women and a much higher number of Chinese and Korean lives. The war also set in motion a number of changes that led to the militarization and intensification of the Cold War.

3 Competition and coexistence, 1950–62

The Korean War (1950–53) transformed the nature of the Cold War and world politics. Its initial impact was to solidify the division of the world into political, military, and economic spheres. Europe remained tense and divided, and the arms race and competition in the Third World emerged as active and fluid aspects of the Cold War. Although the Soviets matched the United States in the development of nuclear weapons and made impressive advances in missile technology, the United States maintained its lead in the arms race. The struggle of the Third World for political independence, economic justice, racial equality, and cultural respect became an increasingly important source of international tension and conflict during the 1950s. Fighting against Western control, Third World countries and movements challenged Western hegemony and provided an opportunity for the expansion of Soviet influence. Soviet–American competition in the Third World intersected with the arms race in 1962 to bring about the Cuban Missile Crisis, the single most dangerous crisis of the Cold War era.

The increased focus on the arms race and the Third World did not mean that Western Europe and Japan were no longer important. One of the greatest challenges the United States faced during the 1950s was how to foster economic growth in Germany and Japan, help them restructure their politics along more or less democratic lines, and integrate them into the Western alliance. The three tasks were interrelated: economic growth and prosperity made democratization and international integration possible.[1] Achievement of economic growth, political stability, and reintegration of these former "rogue" states into the Western alliance was a huge victory for the United States, the West and the capitalist system.

SHIFTING POWER BALANCES

Despite impressive economic and political gains by the Soviet Union, the United States remained by far the stronger of the two superpowers. The world economy almost doubled in size between 1953 and 1963, and although US growth rates lagged behind those of the other major industrial nations (with the exception of Britain), the high growth rates achieved by Western Europe and Japan widened the gap between the West and the rest of the world. Economic growth, in turn, helped alleviate class tensions and undercut the appeal of leftist parties. Economic growth and political stability in Western Europe, West Germany, and Japan, and their integration into the US-led Western alliance enhanced the relative position of the West. In contrast, the Soviets experienced difficulty in maintaining control of Eastern Europe, and the Sino-Soviet alliance, which had joined the two communist giants, began to fall apart at the end of the 1950s.

The Cold War in Europe had largely stabilized by 1950 following the end of the Berlin Blockade, the establishment of separate German states, and the victory of the anti-communist forces in the Greek civil war. Moreover, Marshall Plan aid and covert assistance to anti-communist groups helped ensure the dominance of pro-US parties in Western Europe. Soviet power kept the lid on the much more unsettled conditions in Eastern Europe. Although the two camps maintained massive forces along the East–West divide in central Europe for the rest of the Cold War, only the anomalous situation of West Berlin as a Western outpost deep within East Germany remained a major source of territorial tension between the superpowers in Europe.

The North Korean attack on South Korea, however, raised fears of a similar move by the Soviets in Europe, especially the use of East German forces to attack West Germany. The Truman administration sent four divisions of troops to Western Europe in the fall of 1950, and set in motion the process that turned the North Atlantic Treaty into the North Atlantic Treaty Organization. In place of a political alliance emerged a military organization with an integrated central command structure under US control. This structure not only made coordinated planning against the Soviet threat possible; it also effectively denationalized West European armed forces, making it very difficult for them to be used against each other.

This was especially important in the case of Germany. US military planners believed that rearming West Germany was necessary to ensure the Federal Republic's Western orientation and to gain manpower for the forward defense of Western Europe. In addition, West German leader Konrad Adenauer backed rearmament as a means of regaining sovereignty. The prospect of large numbers of Germans in uniform so soon after World War II shocked US allies, however. After the United States proposed rearming Germany in September 1950, the French responded with a plan for a European Defense Community (EDC). This would integrate limited German forces in small units into a larger West European army. Despite initial doubts, the United States backed the French plan as a way to overcome widespread resistance to German rearmament.

Debate over creation of the EDC stretched out until the summer of 1954 when the French parliament failed to approve the plan. Despite the French action, the Western allies adopted an alternative plan that permitted the Federal Republic to rearm and join NATO in exchange for a pledge not to develop atomic, biological, or chemical weapons. In addition, the United States and Great Britain pledged to maintain forces in West Germany. The Federal Republic joined NATO in May 1955. Shortly thereafter, the United States, Britain, and France formally ended their occupation of West Germany while maintaining a strong military presence there.

West German rearmament and membership in NATO represented a major defeat for Soviet policies toward Germany. The Soviets had tried to head off Western plans to arm West Germany with a series of proposals beginning in the spring of 1952 calling for unification and neutralization of Germany. Convinced that the proposals were merely an attempt to sow confusion in the West, the United States and its allies ignored them and subsequent Soviet calls for German reunification and neutralization.

The combination of US economic strength and technology with German manpower and military prowess was a strategic nightmare for the Soviet Union. To salvage what they could from a bad situation, the Soviets moved in mid-May to formalize their security ties with Eastern Europe by signing a Treaty of Friendship, Cooperation, and Mutual Assistance with Albania, Bulgaria, Czechoslovakia, the German Democratic Republic, Hungary, Poland, and Romania.[2] In combination with West German membership in NATO, this alliance, which became known as the Warsaw Pact, seemed to seal the division of the continent by adding a military dimension to the existing political and economic divisions.

Mainly a reactive and defensive move to maintain the status quo in Eastern Europe, the formation of the Warsaw Pact also precluded the "Austrian option" for the rest of Eastern Europe. A day after signing the Warsaw Pact Treaty, the Soviets ratified the Austrian State Treaty, which ended the allied occupation of Austria in exchange for Austrian neutrality. In addition to removing their occupation forces, the Soviets sold Soviet properties in Austria. Under the post-Stalin leadership of Nikita Khrushchev, the Soviets also sought to mend fences with Yugoslavia. Finally, in September 1955, the Soviets recognized the Federal Republic, and granted the German Democratic Republic control over its foreign affairs, formalizing the division of Germany and Europe. Meanwhile, the leaders of the United States, Great Britain, France, and the Soviet Union had met in July in Geneva. The first high-level meeting between US and Soviet leaders in ten years led to no agreements, but the very fact that such a meeting could take place helped lessen tensions.

Korean War military spending set in motion a prolonged period of economic prosperity in the West that lasted until the early 1970s. US military expenditures ran at around 10 percent of GNP in the 1950s, peaking at 12.7 percent in 1954. Massive military spending generated a high level of aggregate demand and transformed the US economy as military spending shifted the nation's manufacturing base from the northeast and midwest to the southern and western states. Some scholars argue that military spending was not only beneficial but necessary because the key actors in the US political system could not agree on any other form of significant government involvement in the economy. Other scholars point out that military spending came at the expense of domestic reforms, and that in order to gain political support for increased military spending the US government exaggerated the Soviet threat and curtailed civil liberties at home. Military spending maintained demand and economic growth in the short run, but the distorted allocation of resources probably proved harmful in the long run by diverting investment and manpower from the civilian economy.

Military spending also revitalized the Western alliance. Following the end of the Marshall Plan in 1951, US aid to Western Europe continued under the Mutual Security Administration which provided around $25 billion over a four-year period (1951–55). The United States also pumped money into Western Europe with an offshore procurement program under which the US military contracted for some of its supplies in Europe. The Korean War "boom" had an especially strong impact on the West German economy, which had not revived under the Marshall Plan. West Germany was able to take advantage of increased demand due to the existence of spare industrial capacity and an ample supply of skilled and trained labor. Although German militarism did not revive, the West German economic miracle was, to a significant extent, based on the twin foundations of the World War II build-up of German industry and US military spending.

Economic integration also stimulated the West European economy. With the formation of the European Coal and Steel Community in 1951, France, West Germany, Italy, Belgium, The Netherlands, and Luxembourg explicitly surrendered national control over production and use of two raw materials vital to modern industry and warfare to a multinational authority. Western European integration continued with the Treaty of Rome in 1957, which joined the same six countries in a European Economic Community (EEC). (The British decided not to join the EEC, setting up a looser European Free Trade Association.) The EEC eliminated trade barriers among its members, thus creating an economic unit large and efficient enough to compete internationally. Creation of the EEC, with its common tariff on imports, also led to a massive increase in US investment in Western Europe, climbing from $1.7 billion in 1950 to $21.5 billion by the end of the 1960s. While Europeans worried about the American invasion, investment flows coupled with the costs of US troops abroad, tourism, and increased imports led to serious US balance of payments difficulties by the end of the 1950s. Growth rates in that decade averaged around 3 percent a year in Great Britain; 5.9 percent in Italy; and 7.6 percent in West Germany, with the West German share of world exports tripling between 1950 and 1970. Economic growth and increasing international competitiveness allowed the major European states to restore the international convertibility of their currencies at the end of 1958.

Economic growth also underwrote the creation of welfare states throughout Western Europe and the moderation of class conflict, and together with the Cold War led to a decade of center-right hegemony in Western European politics. In 1959, the West German Social Democratic Party (SPD) renounced Marxism, accepted the mixed economy, and ended its opposition to rearmament. Economic integration contributed to better relations among the nations of Western Europe, and by tying the West European economies together made autarkic development and aggression much more difficult.

The Korean War also boosted economic growth and political stability in Japan. Known in Japan as "divine aid," US military expenditure pulled Japan out of the economic stagnation resulting from US-imposed austerity programs. As in Europe, the US special procurement program allowed US armed forces to buy needed supplies locally rather than in the United States. This system pumped around $4 billion into the Japanese economy as the US military bought trucks, uniforms, medical supplies, and a host of other items in Japan for use in Korea, rather than shipping them across the Pacific. Between 1951 and 1956, US military procurement expenditures in Japan paid for over one-quarter of Japan's imports. This massive infusion of US public funds stimulated the struggling Japanese economy. Japanese industrial production increased almost 50 percent between March 1950 and March 1951, and by 1953 manufacturing output stood at more than twice the 1949 level.[3] Growth rates averaged close to 10 percent annually during the 1950s as the government worked closely with business and banking groups to modernize and expand Japanese industry.

The Korean War also changed the political relationship between Japan and the United States. In September 1951, a peace treaty, largely drafted by the United States, formally ended hostilities and restored Japanese sovereignty over the home islands. In separate agreements the United States guaranteed Japanese security, secured the right to military bases in Japan, and retained control over the Ryukyu Islands. By the 1960s, the US base complex on Okinawa, the largest of the Ryukyu Islands, had become key to US offensive and intervention capabilities in the region. In accordance with Article 9 of its 1947 constitution, Japan remained formally demilitarized. The Japanese Self-defense Force, set up during the US occupation, grew to 130,000 troops by 1954, and added air and naval arms. To reassure Japan's neighbors, the United States in 1951 signed a mutual security treaty with the Philippines and entered into a loose alliance with Australia and New Zealand (the ANZUS Pact) which also symbolized US displacement of British influence in the Pacific. The Soviets protested these developments but were powerless to stop them.

Following the Korean War, the United States provided South Korea and Taiwan with massive economic assistance. US economic assistance to South Korea between 1953 and 1962 financed around 70 percent of South Korea's imports and amounted to around 80 percent of total fixed capital formation. In Taiwan, US aid financed almost 40 percent of gross domestic capital formation. The United States also supported land reform in both countries in order to win over the peasantry and to free resources for industrial development. (Unusual circumstances, the replacement of the native Taiwanese elite by Nationalist mainlanders and the disruption caused by the Korean War, facilitated land reform in the two countries.) Economic reform and US aid stimulated rapid economic growth in Taiwan beginning in the late 1950s. South Korean growth rates in the 1950s were lower, but began to rise sharply after a policy shift toward export-led growth following a military coup in 1961.[4]

The Korean War also changed the political relationship between the United States and South Korea and Taiwan. One of Truman's initial actions on June 25, 1950, was to order the US Seventh Fleet into the

Taiwan Strait to defend Taiwan against PRC attack. In 1955, the United States signed a security treaty with Taiwan, and supported it during the Taiwan Strait Crises in 1954–55 and 1958 when the PRC shelled off-shore islands held by Taiwan. The United States also forged a close security relationship with South Korea, and US combat troops remained in South Korea following the war.

In comparison with Western Europe, the situation in Eastern Europe was much less stable. Although vital to Soviet security, the countries of Eastern Europe were also a security problem for the Soviet Union. East European reaction to attempts to liberalize communism demonstrated the depth of anti-Soviet sentiment and the fragility of the Soviet position in the region. As part of the "New Course" following Stalin's death, the Soviets ended the most repressive features of Stalinism in Eastern Europe and backed reformist leaders. Attempts at political liberalization and inconsistent economic policies resulted in strikes and riots in East Germany in June 1953, forcing the Soviets to send in troops to restore control. In a pattern that would be repeated in the rest of Eastern Europe, East Germany was transformed from an aid donor to the Soviet economy to an aid recipient.

At the Twentieth Congress of the Communist Party of the Soviet Union in February 1956, Nikita Khrushchev, who had emerged as Stalin's successor, denounced Stalin and Stalinism in a "secret" speech whose content was leaked to the West. Earlier, in open remarks, Khrushchev had rejected the thesis of inevitable war between communism and capitalism and proclaimed the possibility of peaceful coexistence of states with different social systems. Khrushchev also acknowledged that socialism could come about through parliamentary democracy as well as through revolution.

Rather than gain support for communism, Khrushchev's remarks and efforts to promote reforms in Eastern Europe provoked increased popular discontent in the region. In the summer of 1956, liberalization efforts in Poland threatened to move out of control when the army opened fire on striking workers. With backing from the Chinese, the Polish Communists brought back Władysław Gomułka, a nationalist Communist who had been imprisoned during the purge trials of the early 1950s. Gomułka headed off Soviet intervention by assuring the Soviets that Poland would continue to be a firm ally of the Soviet Union and remain in the Warsaw Pact. Convinced that the Polish people, including the Polish Army, would resist intervention, the Soviets decided to allow Poland to pursue its own path to socialism. Under Gomułka, Poland abandoned collectivization of agriculture, improved relations with the Catholic Church, raised wages, and regained control of its armed forces.

A similar scenario in Hungary led to different results. Following two years of disputes within the Hungarian Communist Party over liberalization, the party, spurred by events in Poland, brought back former party leader Imre Nagy, a nationalist Communist who had been purged during the Stalin years. Nagy was unable to control the momentum of events, and as popular discontent mounted, he announced that Hungary was leaving the Warsaw Pact, proclaimed Hungarian neutrality, and appealed to the United Nations for support. The Soviets made a deal with János Kádár, a prominent Communist who had served a prison term in Stalin's day for nationalist deviation. In return for Kádár's pledge to keep Hungary in the Warsaw Pact, the Soviets agreed to allow Hungary a large degree of latitude in its internal affairs – once Nagy was removed. On November 4, in the midst of the Suez Crisis in the Middle East that was dominating international attention (see below), Soviet and other Warsaw Pact troops re-entered Budapest and brutally crushed the Hungarian revolution.

Although the Chinese and the Yugoslavs supported the intervention, the result was devastating to communist parties in the West, leading to widespread resignations and disillusionment. The intervention also undercut Khrushchev's efforts at liberalization by making it clear that they did not include self-determination for Eastern Europe. On the other hand, the Soviet intervention also demonstrated the hollowness of the "liberation" rhetoric of the Eisenhower administration. With few means short of war to affect the outcome, and its attention focused on the Middle East, the United States limited its response to diplomatic protest.

Soviet reaction to events in Poland and Hungary set limits to political change in Eastern Europe. After restoring Communist Party control, the Soviets relaxed their political and economic pressures on Eastern Europe. In an effort to buy loyalty, the Soviet Union reversed the flow of resources and began subsidizing Eastern European development through increasingly favorable trade arrangements. These policies, coupled with a relaxation of Soviet political controls, resulted in the revival of national communism in Eastern Europe. On the other hand, increased aid to Eastern Europe sharply reduced the amount of aid available for the PRC.

Following the Korean armistice, the Soviets sought to repair relations with the PRC that had been strained during the Korean War. The Soviets backed the PRC in September 1954 when Chinese artillery began shelling the offshore islands of Jinmen and Mazu. The following month, Khrushchev, who was in China to celebrate the fifth anniversary of the revolution, announced the return of the military bases in Lushun (Port Arthur) and the Soviet-run Manchurian railway system to Chinese control and promised generous economic assistance. Then, in April 1955, Khrushchev agreed to help the PRC develop atomic weapons.

Although the Chinese no doubt appreciated these gestures, Sino-Soviet relations began to deteriorate following Khrushchev's secret speech, whose passages attacking Stalin's cult of personality could also be read as criticism of Mao's rule in China. In 1958, the Chinese embarked on the Great Leap Forward, attempting to reduce their reliance on foreign countries by militarizing the economy and accelerating industrialization. The disastrous results, including widespread famine claiming perhaps as many as 30 million lives, undermined Soviet confidence in Mao's leadership. Soviet unease increased when the PRC reignited the dispute over the offshore islands and Taiwan in August 1958, in part to mobilize internal support for the Great Leap Forward. Moreover, Mao, who believed that the Soviet Union was ahead in the arms race, argued that the Soviets should act boldly and not be afraid of a nuclear confrontation with the United States, which he derided as a "paper tiger." Khrushchev, who knew the true state of the strategic balance (see below), limited his support to promises that he would aid the PRC only if the United States attacked China.

Khrushchev also disliked Chinese criticism of his efforts to improve relations with the United States. Chinese pressure on India and the PRC's brutal subjugation of Tibet in 1959 further increased Soviet concerns. In August 1959, Khrushchev halted nuclear cooperation, informing the PRC that the Soviet Union had decided not to provide a prototype atomic bomb as earlier promised. After the Chinese reiterated their belief in the inevitability of war as long as imperialism existed, Khrushchev, in July 1960, decided to withdraw all Soviet military and technical advisers from the PRC.

The Sino-Soviet split made it clear that international communism was neither a monolithic bloc nor a coherent alliance, let alone a viable alternative world order. The United States was slow to recognize the split and to realize its implications, however. At first, US officials feared the split was a sham or, at best, only temporary. After realizing that a key element in the split was Chinese opposition to improved relations between the Soviet Union and the United States, US officials began viewing the PRC as more dangerous than the Soviet Union. Chinese support for national liberation movements and vitriolic anti-American rhetoric further fed American fears.

THE ARMS RACE

While the United States maintained its atomic monopoly (1945–49), US leaders had felt free to rebuild Germany and Japan without fear of war with the Soviet Union. Following the Soviet Union's acquisition of atomic weapons in 1949, the United States sought to maintain nuclear superiority through increased production of atomic weapons and development of the hydrogen bomb. The Korean War led to a massive increase in US military spending. Between 1950 and 1953, the United States expanded its armed forces by over a million troops and dramatically increased production of aircraft, ships, combat vehicles, and other conventional weapons. Only a small part of the increase was directly related to the Korean War. Most was devoted to countering Soviet conventional superiority in central Europe. US leaders believed that a rough balance of power in Europe coupled with nuclear superiority would extend deterrence and preserve US freedom of action all over the world.

Concerned that conventional forces were too costly, and determined to avoid future Korean-type conflicts, the administration of Dwight D. Eisenhower (1953–61) determined to pursue containment "on the cheap" by cutting back conventional forces while threatening to respond to aggression by launching a massive nuclear strike on the Soviet Union. To take care of lesser contingencies, the Eisenhower administration relied heavily on the Central Intelligence Agency, whose covert-action arm had mushroomed in size during the Korean War.

The US nuclear arsenal grew during the Eisenhower administration from around 1,000 warheads in 1953 to approximately 18,000 by 1960. This arsenal included thermonuclear weapons. The United States successfully tested a powerful thermonuclear device in October 1952, and in February 1954 successfully tested an even more powerful, deliverable hydrogen bomb. Work on delivery systems resulted in the development of medium- and intermediate-range ballistic missiles (MRBMs and IRBMs), medium-range bombers, and finally the B-52 transcontinental bomber which entered service in the late 1950s. In September 1955, President Eisenhower approved plans calling for the development of intercontinental ballistic missiles (ICBMs) as the "highest national priority." The United States also began to develop and deploy large numbers of tactical nuclear weapons to compensate for the relative weakness of its ground forces.

Overseas bases were crucial to US strategy. Until the deployment of B-52 intercontinental bombers in the late 1950s and long-range land- and submarine-launched missiles beginning in 1960, the US nuclear deterrent was heavily dependent on bombers that could not reach the

Soviet Union from bases in the United States.[5] This technological real-ity made the United States dependent on bases on the territory of its allies, and helps explain US efforts during the 1950s to ring the Soviet Union and the People's Republic of China with bilateral and regional security pacts. These arrangements enabled the United States to project its power deep inside Soviet and Chinese territory. By the mid-1960s, the United States had 375 military bases in foreign countries and 3,000 other facilities encircling the Soviet Union and its allies.

The Korean War also led to changes in Soviet policies, though the greatest changes came after the death of Stalin in March 1953. As in the United States, the initial impact was increased military spending, and the Red Army swelled from around 2.8 million troops in 1950 to almost 5.8 million by 1955. Stalin's successors, in contrast, wanted to reduce military spending and adopt less confrontational policies toward the West in order to shift economic priorities from heavy industry and military production to light industry, agriculture, and consumer goods. Georgi Malenkov, who became chairman of the Council of Ministers (or prime minister) following Stalin's death, had been associated with the nuclear program and believed that the advent of nuclear weapons made peaceful coexistence both essential and possible. Malenkov was replaced in February 1955, but the new leader, Nikita Khrushchev, adopted a similar program of economic reform and controlled political liberalization. In foreign policy, Khrushchev stressed a defensive orien-tation toward the West, reconciliation with Yugoslavia, and a more active policy toward the Third World.

Stalin's successors cut military spending sharply and in 1955 began a large-scale demobilization of active-duty military personnel. By 1960, Soviet forces were down to around 3.6 million troops. On the other hand, the Soviets continued the development of their strategic nuclear forces, testing a relatively small thermonuclear bomb in August 1953 and a somewhat larger hydrogen bomb in November 1955. Some Soviet writers claim that the Soviet Union was first to develop a hydro-gen bomb because what the United States tested in 1952 was a huge thermonuclear device rather than a deliverable bomb. David Holloway, however, points out that the bomb the Soviets tested in 1953 was not based on the same principles that make "true" hydrogen bombs capable of almost unlimited destructive power.[6]

The Soviets also developed and deployed long-range bombers with the theoretical capacity to reach the United States on one-way missions. Despite US fears of a "bomber gap," the Soviets did not produce long-range bombers in large numbers, turning instead to ballistic missiles. In 1958, the Soviets had only 85 intercontinental bombers compared to

1,769 for the United States; a ratio of almost 22:1 in favor of the United States.[7] In August 1957, the Soviets successfully tested an intercontinental ballistic missile, a feat underlined in October 1957 when they successfully launched *Sputnik*, an earth-orbiting satellite. The Soviets also developed intermediate-range missiles that could reach targets in Western Europe.

Soviet ICBMs transformed the strategic environment by making it possible for the Soviet Union to threaten the United States directly. There was no known means of defending against a ballistic missile attack, and with warning times reduced from hours to minutes, many analysts feared that US nuclear forces, almost entirely bombers, could be decimated in a Soviet surprise attack. Without a guaranteed retaliatory force, the United States would have no credible deterrent. In addition, the new Soviet ability to strike the United States directly also raised concerns that the United States might be reluctant to resist a Soviet attack on Western Europe if in doing so it risked Soviet retaliation against US territory. How to convince its NATO allies that it would stand by them if they were attacked by the Soviet Union became a chronic preoccupation of US strategists.

In the wake of *Sputnik*, many people in the United States feared that the Soviet Union was poised to take the lead in the arms race. Due to a super-secret surveillance program, President Eisenhower knew that the situation was not as serious as it seemed. Beginning in 1956, U-2 spy planes, which flew too high for Soviet anti-aircraft missiles or fighters to stop, mapped and photographed the Soviet Union.[8] From these flights and other information, the United States learned that the Soviet ICBM program was experiencing serious problems. Eisenhower also knew that the United States had plenty of medium-range missiles and bombers in Europe that could strike the Soviet Union, and that US ICBMs would be operational in a few years. (The first US ICBM went on alert in October 1959.) Therefore, he saw no need for massive increases in military spending. In addition, Eisenhower was concerned that overspending on the military would damage the US economy and increase the influence of what he called the "military-industrial complex," the "conjunction of an immense military establishment and a large arms industry."

Nevertheless, pressure mounted for the United States to increase military spending sharply. Although the U-2 flights failed to detect any operational ICBM launch sites, their coverage of the Soviet Union was not complete. In late 1957, the CIA claimed that the Soviets had the ability to build and deploy 500 ICBMs by 1962. In addition, a top-level commission issued a report that warned that US strategic forces were vulnerable to a surprise attack. The report called for a 50 percent increase in US military spending, including over $20 billion for fallout shelters. The "missile gap" became an issue in the 1960 presidential campaign, with the Democrats charging that the Eisenhower administration had allowed the Soviets to gain a dangerous lead in the arms race.

After taking office, President John F. Kennedy (1961–63) convinced Congress to fund a massive increase in US military spending, including a doubling of the Polaris submarine missile program and the Minuteman solid-fueled missile program. Kennedy also put US bomber forces on a crisis footing. Military spending increased by 15 percent between 1960 and 1962, and spending on the space program soared from $400 million in 1960 to $5 billion in 1965. The result of the ongoing and accelerated development and deployment of US strategic weapons systems, coupled with Soviet technical and economic problems, was a massive US lead in strategic weapons.

Shortly before Kennedy took office, a new satellite-based surveillance program began providing greater coverage of the Soviet Union and removed any lingering doubts about US strategic superiority. In February 1961, US Secretary of Defense Robert S. McNamara declared that there was no missile gap. In October, a Defense Department official announced that the United States was aware of the true strength of Soviet strategic forces and pointed out that the arsenal the United States would have left after a Soviet first strike greatly exceeded what the Soviets would possess before such an attack. Indeed, it appeared that the United States had developed sufficient forces for a successful first strike against the Soviet Union.

Kennedy's build-up also called for significant increases in US conventional forces, including the deployment in Europe of several thousand tactical nuclear weapons. NATO forces also grew in size, with West Germany completing its build-up in 1963. US defense officials believed that the strengthening of their conventional forces, including new counter-insurgency forces to deal with instability in the Third World, would enable them to respond flexibly to different levels of threat.

To the Soviets, however, the US build-up looked like the United States was planning to fight a war, including a nuclear war, rather than avoid one. The rocket that had launched *Sputnik* was unsuitable for military use, and the Soviets had limited deployment to only a few missiles. Improved versions were not scheduled to be ready for deployment until 1962. Wanting to cut back military spending in favor of focusing on economic problems, Khrushchev tried to bridge the gap until the newer missiles were ready by a policy of bluff, claiming that the Soviet Union was producing missiles "like sausages." Believing this would deter the United States, Khrushchev announced plans in early 1960 to cut another 1.2 million troops, which would reduce force levels to 2.4 million, the lowest since 1938. Khrushchev argued that ICBMs and nuclear weapons meant that Soviet security was no longer dependent on mass armies. Rather than deter the West, however, Khrushchev's claims stimulated a Western build-up of forces to meet the increased threat.

The US build-up, coupled with the deepening Sino-Soviet split, not only forced Khrushchev to end his cuts but also ended his efforts to revamp Soviet military doctrine. Khrushchev had hoped to rely on ICBMs and cut costly conventional forces in order to devote scarce resources to social and economic programs. Although they continued to have doubts about the reliability of their allies, the Soviets decided to build up the conventional war-fighting capacity of the Warsaw Pact forces. Otherwise, the United States could launch a conventional attack in central Europe under cover of its ICBMs, leaving the Soviet Union with a choice between losing Eastern Europe or a nuclear war with the United States with attacks on the Soviet Union.[9] Khrushchev also ended the moratorium on nuclear testing he had announced earlier, and in October 1961 the Soviet Union detonated a 50–megaton hydrogen bomb.

THE THIRD WORLD

Developments in the Third World were another major source of Cold War tensions. Most of the crises in the Third World in this period grew out of colonialism or other issues that predated the Cold War. Nevertheless, the intrusion of the Cold War exacerbated regional and local struggles as groups in the Third World sought external support and the superpowers looked for allies. In addition, many Third World nations, led by India, Indonesia, and Egypt, sought to define a political space between the two blocs for Third World states to pursue a neutral course in the Cold War. Together with Yugoslavia's non-alignment and the Sino-Soviet split, these efforts, beginning with the Bandung Conference of African and Asian States in April 1955, added a new dimension to transnational ideological conflict.

Radicalized by years of colonial control and repression, many independence movements wanted to nationalize foreign-owned properties, overthrow repressive power structures whether based on traditional practices or on structures of oppression implanted by the colonial powers, and to challenge the West's cultural hegemony through the regeneration of their peoples' customs and culture. Thus decolonization had the potential to bring to power movements hostile to Western capitalism and receptive to statist formulas for rapidly modernizing underdeveloped economies. Such outcomes would not only disrupt the economies and undercut the power of the United States's key allies but could also alter the balance of power and remove vast areas, and their raw materials, markets, and labor forces, from the Western-dominated world economy.

These characteristics of many Third World movements and regimes seemed to align them with the Soviet Union and against the United States. While Lenin had been prepared to support non-communist independence movements in the Third World as part of the global struggle against imperialism, Stalin had limited Soviet support to movements under communist control. Khrushchev, recognizing the opportunities inherent in the Third World's "revolt against the West," tried to gain the support of newly independent, non-communist Third World countries through economic and military assistance. In early 1961, under pressure from the Chinese to demonstrate his revolutionary credentials, Khrushchev announced Soviet support for wars of national liberation. Although many Third World states and movements were happy to accept Soviet assistance, the Soviets gained little lasting advantage from these efforts. Instead, their actions, coupled with continued instability in the Third World, stimulated increased US involvement in the Third World.

The United States had extensive political ties with the Third World, either directly as in Latin America, the Philippines, and South Korea or indirectly through its allies. And, unlike the Soviet Union, the United States had important economic interests throughout much of the Third World. During the 1950s, US policy toward the Third World focused on maintaining the integration of the Third World in the Western-dominated international economy and assuring the Third World's alignment with the West in the Cold War. Increased reliance on imported oil and strategic minerals and the decline of European colonialism made a more active US role seem both desirable and necessary. The United States worked with the Western colonial powers, who were also US allies in the Cold War, to try to control the pace of political and economic change in the Third World. Although for reasons of history, ideology, and enlightened self-interest the United States preferred to work with democratic forces in the Third World, in practice it often sided with monarchs, military dictators, and other anti-democratic but anti-communist elements.

Although the Cold War heightened Western anxieties about social and political change in the Middle East, the crises in the region grew out of Western attempts to maintain their position against indigenous threats rather than threats from Soviet actions. The Iranian Crisis of 1951–53 grew out of Iran's nationalization of the British-owned Anglo-Iranian Oil Company (AIOC) in the spring of 1951. AIOC's Iranian operations were Britain's most valuable remaining overseas asset and the British feared that if Iran succeeded in taking over the company all of Britain's overseas investments would be jeopardized. The United States, which also had extensive overseas investments, opposed the Iranian action. On the other hand, the United States feared that British use of force to reverse nationalization could result in turmoil in Iran that could undercut the pro-Western shah, boost the prospects of the pro-Soviet Tudeh Party, and might even result in intervention by the Soviets at Iranian invitation. Therefore, the United States urged the British to try to reach a negotiated settlement. The British, however, preferred to "stand on their rights," and force Iran to give in by organizing an international boycott of Iranian oil and attempting to manipulate Iranian politics.

US efforts to mediate a settlement failed, as did less public attempts to convince the shah to remove nationalist Prime Minister Muhammad Musaddiq. By 1953, the oil boycott had sharply reduced Iran's export earnings and decimated government revenues. Fearing that Musaddiq might displace the shah and that Tudeh influence was increasing, the United States and Britain covertly organized, financed, and implemented a coup that removed Musaddiq and installed a government willing to reach an oil settlement. Following the coup, US economic and financial assistance helped the shah establish a royal dictatorship, ending the progress Iran had been making toward more representative government.

The Iranian Crisis combined Cold War concerns with efforts by a Third World country to gain greater control over its internal affairs and to break the hold of the Western-dominated world economy. Similarly, the Suez Crisis of 1956 grew out of the Arab–Israeli dispute and Egyptian efforts to finance a massive development project centered on construction of a gigantic dam on the Nile River at Aswan. After Egypt turned to the Soviet Bloc for arms in 1955, the United States and Britain decided to withdraw their support for the Aswan Dam project. Egyptian nationalist leader Gamal Abdel Nasser responded by nationalizing the British- and French-owned Suez Canal Company. The Suez Canal was a major artery of international trade, and the British viewed Nasser's action as an intolerable challenge to their weakening position in the Middle East and the world.

The British, together with the French, who resented Nasser's support for Algerian rebels, and the Israelis, who felt threatened by Nasser's support for guerrilla attacks on their territory, developed a complex scheme to recapture control of the canal through military action. Hoping to minimize US reaction, they attacked in late October, on the eve of US presidential elections. Upset with not being consulted, and concerned about the overall impact on the Western position in the Middle East, the United States opposed the Anglo-French–Israeli action. Using its economic power, the United States forced them to withdraw their forces. The Soviets, who were busy suppressing the Hungarian revolution, played almost no role at all, though they tried to gain Egyptian and Arab favor by issuing threats against the attackers after the United States had already brought the invasion to a halt.

In the wake of the Suez Crisis the United States pledged to protect Middle East states from the Soviet Union and its allies. The crisis in Lebanon that led to US intervention in July 1958 stemmed from internal instability and regional rivalries that had little to do with the Soviet Union. Regionally, US leaders feared the growing influence of Egyptian leader Nasser, whom they viewed as dangerously anti-Western. Within Lebanon, the problem comprised efforts by pro-Western President Kamil Sham'un to stay in power by amending the constitution to allow him to run for a second term. Sham'un's action threatened the internal stability of Lebanese society and resulted in increased opposition to his rule. After a coup by army officers in Iraq in July 1958 overthrew the pro-Western monarchy there, the United States, fearing a similar revolt in Beirut, sent over 14,000 troops to Lebanon and brokered a settlement that maintained the country's pro-Western alignment. The British undertook a simultaneous operation in Jordan to bolster King Hussein.

The Iraqi coup resulted in the withdrawal of Iraq from the Baghdad Pact (Turkey, Iran, Iraq, Pakistan, and Great Britain) which had been organized with US support in 1955 to solidify the "northern tier" of countries separating the Soviet Union from the eastern Mediterranean and the Persian Gulf. The culmination of several schemes to bolster the Western position in the Middle East, the Baghdad Pact, through the inclusion of Pakistan, also further injected the Cold War into the regional rivalry between India and Pakistan. In 1954, in what amounted to an effort to recreate the old Indian Army, the United States had begun supplying Pakistan with military assistance. And, in the same year, Pakistan had joined the US-sponsored Southeast Asia Treaty Organization (SEATO), to gain leverage in its regional rivalry with India.

The ongoing conflict in Vietnam also had roots that reached deeper than the Cold War. While the Vietnamese independence movement, the Viet Minh, was communist-led and supported by the Soviet Union and the People's Republic of China, the war in Vietnam was at its heart a struggle against outside domination. The United States, though urging the French to grant independence to Vietnam, Laos, and Cambodia, had indirectly supported French efforts to regain control of their colonies due to concerns about the stability of the French government, desire to maintain access to Southeast Asian raw materials and markets for European and Japanese reconstruction, and fear of the political impact of "losing" another area to communism. By 1954, the United States, which had begun direct aid to the French forces fighting in Vietnam on the eve of the Korean War, was paying for around 80 percent of the French war effort.

After a disastrous defeat at Dien Bien Phu in the spring of 1954, the French, tired of the costly and unpopular struggle, negotiated their withdrawal at an international conference held in Geneva from May to July.[10] The Geneva settlement provided for the independence of Vietnam, Laos, and Cambodia, with Vietnam divided temporarily at the seventeenth parallel to facilitate the peaceful regrouping of French and Viet Minh forces to the south and north respectively. The Democratic Republic of Vietnam, established by the Viet Minh in 1950, would have control of the area north of the seventeenth parallel, while the pro-Western State of Vietnam would control the southern part of the country. Internationally supervised elections to reunify the country were scheduled to take place in two years.

Although the United States had refused to come to the rescue of the French forces trapped at Dien Bien Phu, it was not ready to accept what it viewed as a communist victory in Southeast Asia. To draw the line against further communist gains, the United States sponsored the formation of SEATO, which pledged its members – the United States, Great Britain, France, Australia, New Zealand, Pakistan, Thailand, and the Philippines – to resist communist aggression in the region. Although not members, Laos, Cambodia, and Vietnam south of the seventeenth parallel were included in the area under SEATO's protection.

Inside Vietnam, the United States sought to build up a non-communist government in the South under the leadership of Ngo Dinh Diem, a prominent non-communist nationalist. US aid, and the support of the nearly 900,000 anti-communist Vietnamese who fled the North, enabled Diem to gain control of the government in the South. Convinced that Viet Minh leader and DRVN head Ho Chi Minh would win reunification elections, the United States, which had refused to sign the Geneva settlement, supported Diem's decision not to participate in the proposed election.

The Viet Minh, who were preoccupied with consolidating their control of the North, protested against Diem's decision but took no action. The Soviet Union and the PRC were also not prepared to go beyond verbal protests. Diem's persecution of his opponents and his reversal of Viet Minh-implemented land reforms soon led to the revival of armed resistance. In 1960, Viet Minh members who had remained in the South, supported by their comrades in the North, organized a broadly based National Liberation Front and embarked on a full-scale military and political struggle to overthrow Diem and reunify the nation.

By this time, the settlement in Laos had also broken down. The royalist government that had taken power in 1954 had formed a neutralist coalition with the communist-led Pathet Lao in 1957. The following year, rightist forces supported by the United States overthrew the neutralist government and adopted a pro-Western position. The neutralists regained control in August 1960, only to lose power to the right again in a December 1960 coup. With the United States supporting the rightist groups, and the North Vietnamese, the Chinese, and the Soviets supporting the left and the neutralists, Laos was in a state of civil war as the new decade began.

An unexpected consequence of the Suez Crisis was to hasten the end of European colonialism in Africa by exposing the vulnerability of the European colonial powers. Morocco and Tunisia had gained their independence in 1956, and in 1957 Ghana became the first sub-Saharan African colony to gain independence. Although Algeria did not become independent until 1962, dissension caused by the war there led to the collapse of the French Fourth Republic in 1958 and the coming to power of a new government, led by Charles De Gaulle, pledged to end the war by granting independence. By 1962, most of Africa, with the notable exceptions of the Portuguese colonies, Southern Rhodesia, and South African-controlled Namibia, had won its independence.

Although the result of a historical dynamic that had little to do with the Cold War, decolonization in Africa was deeply influenced by the international environment dominated by Soviet–American rivalry. Nowhere was this more evident than in the Congo, where Belgium's sudden grant of independence in June 1960 led to a Cold War crisis that significantly shaped the new state's development. Shortly after independence, secessionist forces supported by Belgian and other Western mining interests seized control of the mineral-rich province of Katanga. Dissatisfied by the actions of the United Nations, which sent a peacekeeping force to the Congo but did not assist the central government in regaining control of Katanga, Congolese Prime Minister Patrice Lumumba appealed to the United States and the Soviet Union for help. The United States, suspecting Lumumba of communist sympathies, refused. Although the Soviets sent some assistance, the UN decision to close Congo's airfields to all but UN-approved flights limited what the Soviets could provide. In contrast, covert US assistance to anti-communist Congolese led to Lumumba's removal and replacement by pro-Western military officers. Nevertheless, it took several more years of fighting and US covert aid to secure the Congo and its mineral wealth for the West.

The key issue in Latin America was what kinds of internal political, economic, and social arrangements and external ties would best ensure political stability and economic development. These issues inevitably involved the United States, since it had long sought to control the pace and scope of political and social change in Latin America and to regulate the region's relations with non-hemispheric powers. In the 1950s, the United States sought to increase its influence in Latin America by strengthening its ties with the region's powerful military establishments through a large-scale program of military assistance and training.

As noted earlier, the window of opportunity for political and economic reform that arose during World War II had in most countries been closed before the Korean War. In Guatemala, however, the reformist government that had come to power as a result of the 1944 revolution managed to survive despite the hostility of the US-owned United Fruit Company, which dominated Guatemala's economy. In 1950, free elections brought Jacobo Arbenz, a reform-minded military officer, to power. Two years later Arbenz's government passed land-reform legislation that expropriated several thousand acres of United Fruit property. Arbenz's action confirmed US suspicions that Guatemala was in danger of slipping under communist control. In reality, despite the presence of individual communists in Arbenz's inner circle and in some government agencies, there were only a handful of communists in the legislature and the army remained free from communist influence. Moreover, the Soviet Union took little interest in Guatemala.[11]

Although the receipt of Soviet arms in May 1954 provided an opportunity to condemn Guatemala before the Organization of American States, the United States had already undertaken measures to overthrow Arbenz. The CIA organized, financed, and supported an attack on Guatemala by a small exile army as part of a larger plan to intimidate the Guatemalan Army into removing Arbenz. The plan succeeded, and the leader of the exile army replaced Arbenz. The new government reversed Arbenz's reforms and inaugurated forty years of repressive rule by a succession of military or military-dominated governments that cost over 100,000 Guatemalans their lives and led to the disappearance, and probable death, of another 40,000.

Like Guatemala, the Cuban revolution began as a broadly based indigenous struggle against a corrupt, repressive, US-supported military dictator. And, as in Guatemala, once in power the new Cuban government, which took over in January 1959, soon found itself in conflict with US economic interests that dominated the Cuban economy. Unlike Guatemala, the Cuban government, led by the charismatic Fidel Castro, gained control of the Cuban Army. And, again in contrast with Guatemala, the Soviet Union provided the Cuban revolutionaries with enough economic and military assistance to ensure their survival.

The Cuban revolution came during a period when the United States was trying to adjust to the overthrow of several Latin American military dictatorships and their replacement by civilian governments. Although the collapse of Cuban dictator Fulgencio Batista's regime had caught the United States by surprise, the United States was confident that it could control Cuban developments due to the dependence of the Cuban economy on the United States and the presence of a large, pro-US, professional middle class. As Castro implemented reforms that struck at US economic interests and pro-US Cubans chose exile over resistance, the United States became convinced that stronger measures would be necessary. In addition to economic sanctions that included cutting off Cuban sugar exports to the United States, the Eisenhower administration, in an attempt to repeat its Guatemalan success, organized an invasion force composed of Cuban exiles. Castro, who had received little help from the Soviets during his struggle against Batista, countered the economic sanctions by concluding trade and economic assistance agreements with the Soviet Union. This aid, along with the popularity of the revolution's reforms, Cuban nationalism, and Castro's control of the army, enabled Cuba to defeat the invasion by the US-supported exile force at the Bay of Pigs in April 1961. Following the Bay of Pigs, Castro moved Cuba steadily toward communism and a military alliance with the Soviet Union.

CRISES IN BERLIN AND CUBA

At the same time as the Cuban revolution was being transformed from a revolt against US domination of Cuban society to a major Cold War conflict, a protracted crisis over Berlin was coming to a head. Although West German membership in NATO coupled with the creation of the Warsaw Pact increased order and predictability by lessening uncertainty about the future of Germany and setting limits on permissible behavior, the Soviets remained concerned about Germany. The lack of a formal peace settlement with Germany was a continuing problem, and the Soviets feared that the West was delaying a settlement in the hope that the West German economic "miracle" would pull East Germany and other East European states out of the socialist bloc.

The Soviets also continued to have difficulty constructing a viable state in East Germany. The East German leadership had resisted pressures for reform, and its inhabitants had increasingly reacted to lack of economic and political liberalization by fleeing to the West via West Berlin. The Soviets were also concerned about US plans to furnish West Germany with nuclear weapons delivery systems and feared that the Germans might acquire the weapons themselves. Khrushchev and his generation viewed the Soviet position in Eastern Europe, and especially in East Germany, not only as a strategic imperative but as just compensation for wartime sacrifices, and they were determined not to give it up without a fight.

After the West ignored a plan proposed by the Polish foreign minister to create a nuclear-free zone in central Europe, the Soviets focused on West Berlin, which lay 100 miles inside East German territory, as a way to force the West to recognize the division of Germany and the danger of West Germany acquiring nuclear weapons. In November 1958, Khrushchev proposed a German peace treaty that would recognize the existence of two Germanies. In addition, he called for the end of four-power control of Berlin, with the Western sectors of the city becoming a demilitarized and self-governing free city, its independence guaranteed by the four powers and the two German states. If the West did not agree to these changes within six months, Khrushchev warned, he would turn over control of access routes to the Western sectors of Berlin to the German Democratic Republic.

Although Soviet motives were mainly defensive, Khrushchev's ultimatum led to a crisis. Not only would such a solution run counter to West German claims to represent all of Germany and call into question the Western commitment to reunification, leaving Berlin would deprive the West of a great propaganda asset and an invaluable intelligence listening post and base of operations. Resistance, on the other hand, raised the possibility of war, which, given Soviet superiority in conventional weapons in Europe, could lead to the use of nuclear weapons.

Khrushchev withdrew his ultimatum after Eisenhower invited him to visit the United States in the spring of 1959. Although the two leaders were not able to agree on what to do about Berlin, the meeting sparked hopes on both sides for improved relations and led to progress on negotiations to ban nuclear testing. Hopes for improved relations suffered a blow when the Soviets managed to shoot down a U-2 spy plane on

May 1, 1960, on the eve of a planned summit meeting in Paris. In addition to revealing the most sensitive secrets of the Soviet defense position, the U-2 flights were a humiliating symbol of Soviet technological inferiority. In addition, Chinese criticism put pressure on Khrushchev to show results from peaceful coexistence. When Eisenhower took personal responsibility for the flights and refused to discontinue them, Khrushchev stormed out of the summit before anything could be accomplished.

Khrushchev renewed his ultimatum on Berlin in June 1961 in a tense and contentious meeting with newly elected US President John F. Kennedy in Vienna. Kennedy responded by calling for additional increases in military spending and more funding for civil defense. In a nationally televised address on July 25, 1961, Kennedy pledged that the United States would not let the communists drive the West out of Berlin.

With tensions high, the East Germans, with Soviet approval, sealed off access routes between East and West Berlin on August 13. The tide of refugees fleeing through Berlin had increased during the crisis and had reached 4,000 on the day before the border was closed. The East Germans and Soviets were careful not to interfere with Western access to Berlin. A potentially serious crisis arose in late October when General Lucius D. Clay, whom Kennedy had sent to Berlin to underline US commitment to the city, sent US tanks equipped with bulldozer blades to Checkpoint Charlie, an allied corridor between sectors, to demonstrate US determination to maintain its access rights. Suspecting that the United States was preparing to tear down the wall, the Soviets sent in tanks and a tense confrontation ensued, ending only after an exchange of assurances between Kennedy and Khrushchev.

The Berlin Wall was an ideological defeat of colossal proportions for the Soviet Union and world communism. The wall became a symbol of the Cold War, concrete evidence of the inability of East Germany to win the loyalty of its inhabitants. It was also seen as hard proof that Soviet-style socialism was losing its economic competition with capitalism. Although the wall ended the mass emigration that had been destabilizing East Germany and also led to a period of prolonged stability in Europe, no one at the time knew that this would be the outcome. When a crisis arose in October 1962 over Soviet missiles in Cuba, the initial US reaction was that the Soviets had put the missiles there as a way of forcing the West out of Berlin.

Following the failed Bay of Pigs invasion, the United States had continued its efforts to reverse the Cuban revolution through covert action designed to cripple the Cuban economy through sabotage, assassination plots against Castro and other Cuban leaders, diplomatic efforts to isolate Cuba, and military maneuvers that seemed to be pointing to a US invasion. Aware of all of this, Castro successfully sought increased military assistance from the Soviet Union. In addition, Khrushchev decided to deploy medium- and intermediate-range ballistic missiles in Cuba. Convinced that the United States, which possessed clear naval superiority, would be able to prevent an open deployment of missiles to Cuba, the Soviets tried to deceive the United States about the missiles until they were installed.

The risk of sending missiles to Cuba was taken for several reasons. First, putting missiles in Cuba promised a quick fix to the problem of Soviet strategic inferiority. As noted earlier, both the Soviets and the United States were aware that the United States held a huge lead in strategic weapons. The Soviets feared that such a large lead might tempt US leaders to risk a first strike against the Soviet Union. At the least, the United States might try to exploit its lead by acting more aggressively against Soviet interests, for example, by invading Cuba. Losing Cuba would highlight the political consequences of strategic disparity in an especially embarrassing way and would constitute a tremendous setback for the Soviet Union and world communism. It could even embolden hardliners in the United States who wanted to roll back communism everywhere in the world. Medium- and intermediate-range missiles in Cuba would make a US first strike almost impossible and go a long way toward redressing the Soviet Union's deficiency in ICBMs. The deployment would also allow Khrushchev to continue his plans to shift resources from military and heavy industry to agriculture and the consumer sector. Soviet missiles in Cuba would also be a psychological counter to US missiles in Turkey. Finally, Khrushchev apparently hoped that ending the Soviet Union's massive strategic inferiority would force the United States to respect the Soviet Union and to negotiate a relaxation of tensions.

Khrushchev's gamble almost led to disaster in October 1962 when the United States discovered the deception. A month earlier, Kennedy had warned the Soviets that the United States would not tolerate offensive weapons in Cuba. President Kennedy interpreted the Soviet move as an intolerable challenge to the political, as well as the strategic, status quo. Although not numerous or capable enough to change the overall strategic balance, the forty-two missiles sent to Cuba significantly increased the Soviet Union's ability to strike targets within the United States. In addition, warning times for missiles fired from Cuba would be less than for missiles fired from the Soviet Union due to the shorter distances and to the fact that US early warning systems were designed to detect launches from the Soviet Union. Still, the missiles fell far short of giving the Soviet Union a first-strike capability.

Angry at the Soviets for deceiving him, convinced that he would be impeached if he failed to take action, and concerned that the Soviets would drag out negotiations until the missiles were operational, President Kennedy publicly demanded that the Soviets remove their missiles from Cuba. Although Kennedy rejected calls for air strikes followed by an invasion of Cuba to remove the missiles, he ordered a naval blockade of Cuba as a way of pressuring the Soviets to meet his demands. After several tense days, during which the world was poised on the brink of disaster, Kennedy and Khrushchev reached agreement on a settlement that led to the removal of the missiles as well as several thousand Soviet combat troops and Soviet-supplied tactical bombers in exchange for ending the blockade and a US pledge not to invade Cuba. Recent research has revealed that the United States also secretly agreed to remove nuclear-armed Jupiter missiles from Turkey as part of the understanding that ended the crisis.

The Cuban Missile Crisis dramatically demonstrated the need for Soviet–American cooperation to prevent a nuclear holocaust. Despite its sobering impact, it took the United States and the Soviet Union another decade to act on this insight.

4　From Cold War to détente, 1963–73

The aftermath of the Cuban Missile Crisis ushered in a new stage in the Cold War. Although Soviet–American rivalry remained the dominant feature of the international system and the key areas of conflict continued to be the arms race and the Third World, the dual impact of changes in both areas coupled with the Sino-Soviet split led, in the early 1970s, to Soviet–American détente and Sino-American rapprochement.

Under Presidents John F. Kennedy (1961–63) and Lyndon B. Johnson (1963–69), the United States continued to build up its strategic forces and expand its conventional forces to allow a more "flexible response" to possible communist aggression. The United States also intensified its support of anti-communist governments and groups in the Third World, combining calls for economic development and political reform with greatly increased military assistance, extensive covert activities, and, in the cases of Vietnam and the Dominican Republic, direct military intervention.

Limits to American power became evident by the end of the 1960s. The war in Vietnam had evolved into a costly stalemate, US strategic superiority was eroding, and US economic power was declining in relative terms as the economies of Western Europe and Japan continued to outperform that of the United States. President Richard Nixon (1969–74) attempted to halt the decline in US power through a policy of détente with the Soviet Union that included arms control, an opening to China, and a reliance on regional allies in the Third World. Nixon also revamped US foreign economic policy.

In October 1964, a triumvirate composed of First Secretary Leonid Brezhnev, Chair of the Council of Ministers Aleksei Kosygin, and President Nikolai Podgornyi replaced Soviet leader Nikita Khrushchev. Khrushchev's attempts at economic reform had failed, his political and administrative reforms had alienated large numbers of party bureaucrats, and his erratic foreign policy leadership had led to near disaster over Cuba and a deepening rift with the People's Republic of China. The new leaders made an effort to increase economic efficiency and improve living standards, halted but did not reverse de-Stalinization, and undertook a massive military build-up that enabled the Soviet Union to achieve strategic parity with the United States in the 1970s. The Soviets were not able to repair relations with the PRC, which continued to worsen, or to stabilize the situation in Eastern Europe. Nevertheless, Brezhnev, who had emerged as first among equals by the end of the decade, was able to reach arms control and other agreements with the United States that stabilized relations between the two superpowers and improved Soviet security.

SHIFTING POWER BALANCES

Shortly after the Cuban Missile Crisis, Khrushchev sent Kennedy a personal letter calling for renewed efforts to conclude a nuclear test ban treaty. Negotiations for a test ban had been going on since the late 1950s, but were deadlocked on the issue of verification. Some US scientists and others feared that without extensive onsite inspections, which the Soviets opposed, it might be possible to conduct underground nuclear tests that could not be detected by technical means. It proved impossible to resolve these differences, so both sides abandoned the goal of a comprehensive test ban and accepted an agreement that prohibited all nuclear testing in the atmosphere, underwater, and in outer space. The Limited Test Ban Treaty, which went into effect in October 1963, addressed the problem of nuclear fallout from atmospheric testing, but it did not stop the arms race, as underground testing continued.

During the 1960s, the United States continued building up its strategic forces. Although the number of US missile launchers leveled off by the end of the decade, technical progress enabled the United States to build more accurate missiles, and, in the second half of the decade, to develop multiple independently targetable re-entry vehicles (MIRVs), multiple warheads on a single missile capable of being aimed at separate targets. The US nuclear stockpile peaked in 1966 at about 32,200 nuclear warheads, while the number of US tactical nuclear weapons in Europe almost tripled to 7,200 during the 1960s.

As the Soviet nuclear arsenal grew, some US strategists began to downgrade the importance of numerical superiority and espouse the doctrine of assured destruction. Labeled mutually assured destruction (MAD) by its critics, the idea behind assured destruction was to convince the Soviets that an attack on the United States would result in nuclear retaliation and the assured destruction of both sides. Assured destruction never became the basis for US targeting strategy, which remained focused on Soviet nuclear forces, but it provided a conceptual basis for limiting strategic weapons since only a small number of nuclear weapons would be needed to cause unacceptable damage.

During the 1960s, nuclear strategy and nuclear sharing became key issues in NATO. Some Europeans feared that the build-up of NATO's conventional forces could tempt the United States to accept a limited war in Europe and not to risk using its nuclear deterrent against the Soviet Union. The United States, for its part, was concerned that British and French possession of nuclear weapons (France successfully tested an atomic bomb in 1960) would dilute US influence in NATO and might tempt the West Germans to demand nuclear weapons for themselves. The United States tried to address both problems by proposing a multi-lateral nuclear force composed of a small seaborne nuclear missile force controlled by NATO and manned by multinational crews. Since all NATO members would have to agree on the launching of these weapons, the United States would retain a veto on their use. This was unacceptable to the French, and no agreement was ever reached. Britain and France kept their nuclear forces, and West Germany remained non-nuclear.

French leader Charles De Gaulle viewed an independent French nuclear force, the *force de frappe*, as a key element in restoring France's status as a great power. During the 1960s, France pursued an increasingly independent foreign policy. In 1963, De Gaulle vetoed Britain's application for membership of the European Economic Community and signed a Friendship Treaty with West Germany, which committed the two nations to close cooperation in foreign policy. The following year France broke ranks with the United States and established diplomatic relations with the People's Republic of China. (Although France did not break relations with the Republic of China, the Taiwan government reacted by breaking relations with France.) De Gaulle also tried to improve relations with the Soviet Union. In 1966, he withdrew French forces from NATO's integrated military command and demanded that all foreign troops be withdrawn from French territory, forcing NATO to move its headquarters from Paris to Brussels. France did not leave NATO, however, and NATO plans continued to assume that French forces would be available in the event of a Soviet attack.

In a May 1967 agreement with the United States and Great Britain, West Germany agreed to cover a larger portion of the foreign exchange costs of US and British forces stationed in its territory. The agreement helped relieve pressures for the withdrawal of US and British forces from West Germany. By 1967, NATO's conventional forces had been sufficiently strengthened that the alliance officially endorsed the strategic doctrine of flexible response. Rather than depending on the intimidating effect of the US strategic arsenal to deter Soviet aggression, flexible response emphasized forward defense and conventional warfighting capacity, with nuclear weapons reserved for use should conventional defense prove inadequate. At the same time, NATO also adopted a report that concluded that "military security and a policy of détente are not contradictory but complementary." The report called on the Western allies to use NATO as the key institution through which the United States and Western Europe could seek a new relationship with the Soviets and Eastern Europe.

In Western Europe, the members of the European Economic Community, or Common Market, submerged old animosities and focused on economic integration and growth. Japan averaged an annual growth rate of around 10 percent during the 1960s. Japan's share of global GNP rose from 5.7 percent in 1964 to 12.9 percent in 1973. A key factor behind Japan's success was the US war in Vietnam. (The fastest period of economic growth came in the period 1966–70, the period of peak US involvement in the Vietnam War.) As it had during the Korean War, Japan became an industrial base for the US war effort, providing over $1 billion a year in military supplies and services. US expenditures in Southeast Asia, South Korea, and Taiwan also created markets for Japanese exports. Profits earned as a result of the Vietnam War helped Japan modernize its industry, develop new technology, and finance investments in raw materials. By the end of the 1960s, Japan had replaced the United States as the leading economic power in Southeast Asia and Japanese exports were on their way to becoming a major force in US markets.

Like Japan, Taiwan supplied a large variety of goods for the US effort and benefitted enormously from exports to Vietnam under the US-financed Commercial Import Program. Taiwan also profited by sending experts and advisers, paid with US funds, to Vietnam, and earnings from the war lessened the impact of the phasing out of US foreign assistance in 1965. South Korea sent combat troops to Vietnam as well as civilian specialists, all paid by the United States, and supplied goods. By 1969, around 20 percent of South Korea's foreign exchange earnings derived from Vietnam-related activities. The Vietnam War helped Taiwan and South Korea make the transition from inward-looking economic policies to a development strategy stressing exports. Economic growth in South Korea, which had averaged around 4 percent per year from 1953 to 1960, jumped to nearly 10 percent in the 1960s.

During the 1960s, the Soviet economy achieved real though faltering economic growth and a gradual improvement in living standards. The Soviet economy had grown at an annual rate of 6.4 percent between 1950 and 1958; the rate fell to 5.3 percent between 1958 and 1967, and to 3.7 percent between 1967 and 1973. The Soviet economy was still much smaller than the US economy (50 to 75 percent smaller), and suffered from technological backwardness (except in the military sector), low productivity, poor quality, and chronic shortages. Agriculture remained a major area of weakness, and as living standards rose, the Soviet Union became dependent on grain imports. The new leadership recognized that improved efficiency was necessary for raising living standards, maintaining legitimacy, and increasing defense spending. Efforts to enact economic reforms were frustrated by government bureaucrats, however, forcing the Soviet Union to look to trade with the West as a way out of its economic impasse.

One of the main lessons the Soviets drew from the Cuban Missile Crisis was the need to augment their strategic capabilities in order to avoid future humiliations. The US military build-up, increasing US intervention in Vietnam, and deteriorating relations with China also contributed to the decision to build up Soviet military power. Following the missile crisis, the Soviet Union decided to embark on a costly military build-up designed to erode US strategic superiority and develop a significant naval presence. Between 1965 and 1970, Soviet military spending rose by around 40 percent. Such levels of military spending strained the economy, but, with memories of the devastation wrought by World War II still fresh, the Soviet leadership was prepared to pay a high price for security.

The results of the build-up were first evident in strategic weapons. The new generation of ICBMs that began to be deployed in large numbers after 1965 gave the Soviet Union the virtually certain capability to inflict heavy damage on the United States in a retaliatory strike. This achievement raised the possibility that nuclear war could be avoided as the ability of each side to inflict unacceptable damage on the other might prevent both from using nuclear weapons. This, however, meant that the possibility of a conventional war could not be ruled out. To avoid losing such a conflict, especially given the improvements in NATO's conventional forces under the rubric of flexible response, Soviet strategists believed that it would be necessary to defeat NATO forces in Europe in order to deny the United States bases from which it could mount a conventional attack on the Soviet Union. Therefore, in addition to building up their strategic forces, the new Soviet leadership reversed Khrushchev's plans to reduce conventional forces and began an expensive expansion and modernization of their conventional capacity.[1]

The new strategy underlined the importance of the Soviet military presence in Eastern Europe and precluded radical departures in Soviet relations with the region. Despite a relaxation of political controls and increasing trade subsidies, the communist regimes of Eastern Europe were still fragile and the Soviet Union could not count on the loyalty of the region. In the 1960s, Romania began to pursue an increasingly independent foreign policy, expanding its trade with the West and at times refusing to participate in Warsaw Pact military maneuvers. The Romanians never threatened to leave the Warsaw Pact, however, and communist dictator Nicolae Ceauşescu kept an iron grip on internal dissent.

Although the Soviets tolerated Romania's deviation, they were not so flexible when efforts by a reformist communist government in Czechoslovakia to build "socialism with a human face" threatened to get out of control. In August 1968, Warsaw Pact troops representing the Soviet Union, Hungary, Poland, and Bulgaria invaded Czechoslovakia, removed the reformers, and restored hardline communist control. Although the reformers had promised that Czechoslovakia would remain in the Warsaw Pact and had tried to keep control of the pace of reforms, the Soviet leadership feared the reforms could undermine communist control throughout the region and threaten their East European security zone. Unlike Romania, Czechoslovakia lay at the center of Eastern Europe, forming a strategic corridor between the West and the Soviet Union. Even a neutral Czechoslovakia would split the region and complicate its defense.

The Soviets sought to justify their action by asserting the right of the Soviet Union to intervene in other communist countries to maintain their "socialist" orientation, both internally and internationally. Labeled the Brezhnev Doctrine by the Western press, the Soviet statements underlined the extent to which Soviet leaders still believed that only communist regimes would respect Soviet security needs and the lengths to which they would go to maintain a security zone in Eastern Europe.

Even more than their earlier intervention in Hungary, Soviet intervention in Czechoslovakia severely damaged the international reputation of communism and the Soviet Union. In addition, the crushing of the Prague Spring was a defeat for reformers in the Soviet Union and Eastern Europe, and led to the abandonment of reform plans throughout the region. Although the United States and NATO temporarily postponed arms control talks and a planned summit, the reimposition of control in Czechoslovakia might have been a prerequisite for détente because it set limits on Eastern Europe's freedom of action, limits without which the Soviets might not have risked détente.

Even communist control did not guarantee loyalty to the Soviet Union, however. Already evident by the late 1950s, the Sino-Soviet split opened to a chasm in the 1960s with the escalation of ideological and territorial disputes. The Chinese not only challenged Soviet leadership of international communism but made significant claims on Soviet territory in Central Asia and the Far East. Underestimating the geopolitical and domestic concerns underlying Chinese hostility, the new Soviet leadership initially blamed Khrushchev for the problems with the PRC. Soviet efforts to revive the old relationship ended in failure, however, and convinced the new leadership that it would not be possible to mend the split.

Chinese hostility greatly complicated the Soviet strategic position, forcing Soviet military planners to increase their forces along their long land border with the PRC. Between 1961 and 1971, the number of Soviet troops along the border more than tripled, and the Soviets greatly increased the number of aircraft and ballistic missiles targeted on the PRC. The PRC's successful test of an atomic bomb in October 1964, a ballistic missile with a live warhead in October 1966, and a hydrogen bomb in June 1967 greatly increased the demands on the Soviet military as they now had to devise defenses against Chinese nuclear weapons as well as those of the West.[2]

TURMOIL IN THE THIRD WORLD

The Sino-Soviet split weakened the Soviet Union and constituted a momentous shift in the global balance of power. Initially, however, its impact was masked by the growth of Soviet military power and turmoil in the Third World. As in the 1950s, the main sources of instability and conflict in the Third World often had little to do with either the United States or the Soviet Union. But, as in the 1950s, instability and conflict in the Third World increased Cold War tensions. Likewise, the involvement of the superpowers exacerbated local and regional problems.

The Cuban revolution highlighted the potential for revolutionary upheaval in Latin America. Although conditions varied widely in the region, Latin America as a whole suffered from an extremely uneven distribution of income, especially glaring inequalities in land ownership (as a general rule, 5–10 percent of the people owned 70–90 percent of the land), limited social mobility, and crushing poverty. In addition, Latin American nations typically had underdeveloped infrastructures, unstable prices for their main exports, declining terms of trade, and limited capital investment. To make matters worse, conservative elites and their military backers opposed widespread aspirations for social, economic, and political reform.

The US response to the Cuban revolution reflected two divergent interpretations of what had happened in Cuba. One theory held that poverty, political repression, and lack of reform had caused the revolution. The other maintained that Castro had come to power because the Cuban Army had collapsed. According to the first view, the way to prevent future Cubas was to promote economic development and political reform through foreign aid. The second view maintained that the way to prevent communists from taking power was to build up Latin America's armed forces.

The Alliance for Progress, announced by President Kennedy in March 1961, was based on the first view. Kennedy proposed a ten-year program to promote economic growth, social reform, and political democracy. An inter-American conference in Uruguay in August set specific goals, including land and tax reform, improved education, health care, and housing, and a per capita growth rate of 2.5 percent per year. The United States pledged to provide a major part of the $20 billion in foreign aid and investment that would be needed to achieve these goals.

US economic assistance and private investment increased substantially during the 1960s, though bilateral economic aid dropped sharply in the second half of the decade. In all, Latin America received over $22 billion in economic assistance and foreign investment during the decade of the Alliance. The net transfer of resources was considerably lower, however, because Latin American countries transferred significant amounts to First World countries to service accumulated debts and repatriate profits from foreign companies operating in Latin America. Nevertheless, Latin American economic growth in per capita terms increased from 2.1 percent per year during the 1950s to 2.4 percent during the 1960s, and climbed to 3.7 percent in the early 1970s.

Although most countries made considerable progress, the social goals of the Alliance – improved health, education, and housing – proved more difficult to achieve. Land reform proved especially intractable as a combination of elite resistance and the centralizing tendencies of commercial agriculture prevented significant land reform anywhere in the region. In addition, the US Congress was reluctant to provide funding for land reform.

The record of the Alliance for Progress in the political realm was even worse. As one scholar notes, "instead of promoting and consolidating reformist civilian rule, the 1960s witnessed a rash of military coups."[3] Although military coups were a common feature of the region's history, a key factor behind the increasingly active role of the military in Latin America in the 1960s was US military assistance and training. Determined to prevent another Cuba, the United States poured millions of dollars into counter-insurgency training and civic action programs, greatly enhancing the ability of the region's military establishments to dominate their societies. Initially critical of military coups, the United States soon began to view military regimes as bulwarks against insta-bility and revolution. By 1964, the United States had abandoned any pretense of favoring social and political reform and focused instead on opposing communism, protecting US private investment, and promot-ing economic growth.

The new policy received its first test in Brazil. Concerned that the center-left government was moving too far to the left, the United States encouraged and supported the government's opponents and wel-comed its overthrow by military officers in the spring of 1964. The new government brutally imposed its control, crushing political parties and trade unions, and adopted a pro-US foreign policy. The United States, which had been ready to assist the coup if needed, increased its economic and military assistance to Brazil. The Brazilian military regime became the archetype of a new type of military regime, extremely repressive and obsessed with internal security and economic development. By the end of the decade most Latin Americans lived under right-wing authoritarian governments.

In 1965, the United States, fearing a repeat of the Cuban debacle, rushed over 28,000 troops to the Dominican Republic when the local military proved unable to defeat a popular revolt aimed at reinstating the constitutionally elected president, whom the military had overthrown in 1963. In a statement that predated the Brezhnev Doctrine by three years, President Johnson justified his action by asserting that the American states would not permit any nation in the Western Hemisphere to fall to communism.[4]

Regional dynamics were especially important in the Middle East where they combined with the Cold War concerns of the superpowers to produce a very violent and potentially explosive mixture. The main regional issue was the Arab–Israeli dispute, though inter-Arab rivalries were also important. Because of its proximity to the Soviet Union's southern border, the Middle East was very important to Soviet security, and the main Soviet objective was to exclude US military bases from the region. The primary US interest in the Middle East was oil. Although the United States imported only small amounts of Middle East oil, Western Europe and Japan had by the 1960s become heavily dependent on oil imports from the region. The US interest in bases in the Middle East and in the security of conservative, pro-Western regimes in the region were largely derivative of its primary interest in oil. Finally, the United States also had a deeply felt, but until mid-decade largely emotional, commitment to the security of the state of Israel.

Due to their divergent interests in the region, the United States and the Soviet Union found themselves supporting, and arming, different sides in the regional dispute. The Soviets backed radical Arab regimes that were anti-Western as well as hostile to Israel. In addition to supporting the conservative monarchical governments of the region's major oil-producing states the United States, despite fears of alienating the region's Muslim majority, including conservative US allies, gradually became the chief arms supplier to Israel.

The 1967 Middle East War proved to be an important turning point in the Cold War in the Middle East as well as in the Arab–Israeli dispute. The war was over in six days as the Israelis struck swiftly and crushed Egyptian, Syrian, and Jordanian forces. After the war, the Israelis occupied the Golan Heights, the West Bank of the Jordan River, Old Jerusalem, and the Sinai. Although the United States and the Soviet Union stayed out of the fighting, after the war each moved closer to their respective allies. The Soviets increased their support for the radical Arab states, providing arms and military advisers to Egypt, Syria, and Iraq. The Soviets also spent billions to develop port facilities in Egypt to support their naval presence in the eastern Mediterranean. The United States began to view Israel as a strategic asset, a bulwark against the Soviet Union and its clients and a bastion of order in the region. To ensure continued Western access to the region's oil, the United States simultaneously strengthened its ties with Saudi Arabia and Iran.

The Cold War also continued to influence African developments. After the independence wave of the early 1960s the key issue in Africa was the future of Portugal's colonies and the white-minority regimes in South Africa and Southern Rhodesia, the latter of which unilaterally declared independence from Britain in 1965. While aware that white racism and repression radicalized black Africans, US officials feared that turning power over to the black majority risked instability and opened the door to communist inroads. The United States also had significant strategic and economic interests in sub-Saharan Africa. Southern Africa was a major source for such strategic minerals as uranium, cobalt, chromium, and manganese. In addition, with the development of supertankers too large to use the Suez Canal, an increasing portion of Middle East oil exports used sea lanes that ran along the east coast of Africa and around the Cape of Good Hope. Similarly, the

United States was extremely reluctant to oppose Portugal's efforts to hold on to its colonies due to fears of losing access to vital airfields in the Portuguese Azores.

The United States also continued to intervene in the Congo, covertly financing white mercenaries supporting the pro-Western government and providing aircraft to transport Belgian paratroopers in 1964. Generally, however, the United States preferred to let local groups or the ex-colonial powers take the lead in maintaining Western influence in Africa. Although the Soviets maintained ties with radical groups in southern Africa, the Portuguese and the white minority regimes in South Africa and Rhodesia appeared in control of the situation. As the 1970s began, the Nixon administration predicated its policies toward the region on the assumption that "the whites are here to stay."

VIETNAM AND THE ORIGINS OF DÉTENTE

US involvement in Vietnam began in the late 1940s as an attempt to shore up a beleaguered France and to secure markets and raw materials for a rebuilding Japan. In the 1950s, the United States committed itself to guaranteeing the survival of a non-communist state in Vietnam south of the seventeenth parallel. US leaders feared that the loss of South Vietnam to communism would initiate, in President Eisenhower's memorable phrase, a "falling domino" effect that would lead to communist control of all of Southeast Asia and threaten Japan. Viewing efforts by Vietnamese communists to overthrow the US-backed government of South Vietnam as a case of communist aggression, rather than as the continuation of the internal struggle for power in Vietnam, US policymakers argued that what was at stake was not merely Vietnam but the credibility of US commitments all over the world.

By the early 1960s, the government of South Vietnam was in trouble as communist-led forces (organized as the National Liberation Front or NLF, but known to American troops as the Viet Cong) began to score military victories and control more and more territory. The United States reacted to the growing threat by sending increasing numbers of US troops to Vietnam. When Kennedy took office in 1961, there were around 600 US military advisers in Vietnam. By the time he died in November 1963, the US troop total exceeded 16,000.

The South Vietnamese government under Ngo Dinh Diem rested on a narrow social base of wealthy landowners, French-educated civil servants, and Catholics, who made up less than 20 percent of the population. Although the United States pushed Diem to undertake social, political, and military reform, he resisted, and the war continued to go badly. After Diem brutally repressed Buddhist opposition to his rule, he was ousted, and killed, in early November 1963, by high-ranking military officers acting with the blessing of US officials.

Diem's successors were no more representative and even less successful in prosecuting the war than he had been. In March 1965, the United States began sending combat troops to Vietnam in order to prevent a communist victory. US combat troops and a US bombing campaign against the North were unable to defeat the NLF and end the war. Massive firepower and US pacification programs destroyed local community structures and depopulated the countryside without winning the allegiance of the population. The result was a costly and bloody stalemate. By 1968, the number of US troops in Vietnam had reached 535,000.

While the United States observed few limits in its conduct of the war in South Vietnam, it stopped short of invading the North due to fear of Chinese intervention, as in the Korean War. In the period 1965–68, the PRC deployed around 50,000 troops in North Vietnam, providing logistical support and acting as a deterrent to an American invasion. Recent research has revealed that the PRC warned the United States that an invasion of North Vietnam would result in Chinese intervention. To underline their seriousness, the Chinese undertook an extensive and expensive civil defense program to prepare the nation for a possible war with the United States.

The Soviets supported North Vietnam with generous military aid that matched growing US involvement in the war. The Soviets also provided training for North Vietnamese forces and helped organize North Vietnam's air defense system. Ironically, the Sino-Soviet split may have aided the North Vietnamese as the Soviets and the Chinese competed to aid them. Neither would halt aid, as this would be seen as helping the American "imperialists." The Soviets, in particular, felt pressure to demonstrate their revolutionary credentials by providing more and more aid to North Vietnam. On the other hand, the Soviets also wanted to improve relations with the United States and worked throughout the 1960s to promote a negotiated settlement of the war. Likewise, the PRC's leaders came to realize that aiding North Vietnam undercut their interest in gaining US support against the Soviet Union.

By the end of the decade, the strategic, economic, and political costs of treating Vietnam as a vital country in the global containment of communism were proving too great for the United States. Many US defense planners were becoming alarmed at the war's drain on US resources at a time when the Soviets were expanding their nuclear forces.

The Vietnam War had also begun to damage the American economy, feeding inflation and driving up the budget deficit. In 1968, the US budget deficit reached $24.2 billion, approximately the cost of the Vietnam War for that year. Unlike earlier twentieth-century wars, the Vietnam War occurred during a period of prosperity and robust economic activity in the United States. Increased military spending, rather than pulling the country out of recession or depression, as in earlier wars, fueled inflation. In addition, the war's costs exacerbated US balance of payments problems, putting enormous pressure on the nation's gold reserves. And, rather than reassuring US allies about the reliability of US commitments, the intervention in Vietnam fed doubts about US foreign policy priorities. None of the United States's European allies sent troops to fight alongside the US forces in Vietnam. Finally, the war's growing unpopularity at home had begun to undermine the popular consensus supporting US foreign policy, and to fuel the growth of an anti-war movement.

The Tet Offensive by communist forces in early 1968 brought these problems to a head. Although US forces repulsed the offensive and inflicted heavy casualties on the attackers, the very fact that the communists could mount such a powerful challenge after three years of US military effort demonstrated that the war was far from being won. Moreover, the Tet Offensive coincided with a severe balance of payments crisis that underlined the economic costs of the war and contributed to President Johnson's decision to cap the US military commitment and try to negotiate an end to the fighting. Tet also forced Johnson to withdraw from the presidential elections and helped propel Richard Nixon, who claimed he had a secret plan to end US involvement in Vietnam "with honor," into the White House.

Nixon's plan to get the United States out of Vietnam was part of an overall revision of US grand strategy that also included arms control, relaxation of tensions with the Soviet Union, rapprochement with China, and reductions in direct US military involvement in the Third World by devolving policing functions onto regional powers armed and aided by the United States. As for Vietnam, Nixon and his national security adviser, Henry Kissinger, hoped that rapprochement with the Soviet Union and China would dilute their support for North Vietnam and force the communists to negotiate an end to the war.

Nixon and Kissinger believed a new strategy was necessary because the erosion of US strategic superiority over the Soviet Union had been accompanied by challenges to US economic hegemony from Western Europe and Japan. In addition, the Vietnam War and the Sino-Soviet split had undermined the previously unchallenged verities of containment and had severely strained, or perhaps shattered, public support for an interventionist foreign policy. Economic incentives and the threat of a strategic partnership with the PRC would serve to restrain the Soviet Union, and arms control would protect US security while reducing costs and the risk of war. Finally, trade with the Soviets, Eastern Europe, and the PRC held out the prospect of overcoming some of the long-standing economic difficulties exacerbated by the war, especially since US competitors traded extensively with the communist countries.

The Soviets wanted to improve relations with the United States. They sought to stabilize the arms race at a rough parity before a new US technological surge left them behind once more. In addition, the Soviets faced mounting economic problems, and wanted to increase trade with the West, especially in grain and advanced technology. They also wanted to gain international recognition of the status quo in central and Eastern Europe and of the Soviet Union as a global power. Due to their increased military power and the negative impact of the Vietnam War on US global power, the Soviets believed that the global correlation of forces had turned in their favor. In particular, they believed that approaching parity in nuclear weapons ended the need to defer to the United States and entitled the Soviet Union to increased political influence, including an equal right to intervene in the Third World.

Finally, Chinese hostility gave the Soviets a powerful incentive to improve relations with the West. Fearful of a US–Chinese alliance, the Soviets hoped to neutralize the threat of collusion by giving the United States a greater stake in good relations with the Soviet Union. The Soviets viewed the fighting along the Sino-Soviet border in 1969 as proof that the Chinese had designs on Soviet territory. Relaxation of tensions with the West reduced the threat of conflict on two fronts and held out the prospect of isolating the PRC and delaying its military development.

The Chinese were also ready to improve relations with the United States. The Soviet invasion of Czechoslovakia in 1968 had shaken the Chinese, and the Brezhnev Doctrine raised the specter of a similar Soviet-led attack on the PRC. Indeed, the Chinese may have initiated the incidents that led to full-scale fighting along the Sino-Soviet border in 1969 as a way of demonstrating that they would resist Soviet pressure. Despite dissent within the Chinese leadership, Mao had become convinced of the necessity of improving relations with the United States as a way to deter Soviet aggression.

It was not easy for the United States to normalize relations with the PRC. The economic and logistic support the Soviets and the PRC provided North Vietnam masked the significance of the Sino-Soviet split and seemed to show that old communist bloc loyalties were still paramount. Even after clear evidence of the split had emerged in the mid-1960s, the United States tended to see the split as proof that the Chinese had become more radical and dangerous than the Soviet Union. The PRC supported revolutionary groups in the Third World, and the Cultural Revolution, though primarily internal in thrust, was accompanied by militant anti-American as well as anti-Soviet rhetoric. Moreover, the PRC refused to adhere to the 1963 Limited Test Ban Treaty and denounced the 1968 Nuclear Non-proliferation Treaty (see below) as an attempt to perpetuate the superpowers' near monopoly of nuclear weapons.

By the end of the 1960s, however, the United States began to recognize that rapprochement with the PRC offered an opportunity to maintain its dominant position in world politics that had been shaken by the Vietnam War and the Soviet strategic build-up. Despite the acquisition of nuclear weapons and the development of delivery systems, Chinese military capacity had declined in relative terms since the 1950s, and the United States no longer regarded the PRC as a major military threat. In addition, the excesses of the Cultural Revolution had diminished the appeal of Chinese communism as a development model. Moreover, the Sino-Soviet split concentrated Chinese attention on its northern border, thus lessening pressure on nations to the south. De-escalation in Vietnam implied a change in US policy toward the PRC because a key objective of US policy toward Vietnam had been to contain Chinese expansion. As the United States wound down its direct role in Vietnam after 1968, the PRC also began withdrawing its troops from the country.

The 1965 military coup in Indonesia also eased fears that Southeast Asia's largest country might fall to communism. Although it appears that the United States was not directly involved in the events that led to the replacement of Indonesian nationalist leader Achmed Sukarno and a bloodbath in which as many as 500,000 Indonesian communists and others died or disappeared, US officials had for years been urging the Indonesian military to replace Sukarno. The United States welcomed the coup and assisted the Indonesian military in tracking down suspected communists.

Trying to link détente with progress toward settlement in Vietnam delayed both. It took Nixon and Kissinger four years to negotiate US withdrawal from the war. Meanwhile, the killing continued, the war spread into Cambodia and Laos, and the economic and political costs of the war mounted. By the time the last US combat forces left Vietnam in early 1973, almost 59,000 US servicemen and women had died. Estimates of Vietnamese deaths reach 3 million. In August 1971, with both the budget deficit and the balance of payments deficit mounting, Nixon imposed a freeze on wages and prices, a surcharge on imports, and effectively took the United States off the gold standard by announcing that the US government would no longer make gold available for dollars. Nixon's action allowed foreign exchange rates to float and devalued the dollar, setting in motion the end of the Bretton Woods system that had governed the global financial order since World War II.

SUPERPOWER DÉTENTE

The Soviets had been ready as early as the spring of 1968 to begin arms control talks with the United States. In what was in many ways a preventive move to limit the spread of nuclear weapons before reducing their own arsenals, the United States and the Soviet Union had, on July 1, 1968, signed the Nuclear Non-proliferation Treaty. In particular, the Soviets wanted to ensure that West Germany did not acquire nuclear weapons. Although the Soviet intervention in Czechoslovakia was a factor in delaying the onset of strategic arms limitation talks (or SALT), the Soviets were reluctant to begin negotiations until the Federal Republic signed the Non-proliferation Treaty in late November 1969.

The Soviets also made West German adherence to the Non-proliferation Treaty a prerequisite for détente in Europe. Europe had been a central focus of the Cold War from its beginning, and even as other areas came into prominence Europe remained the central locus of East–West confrontation. As West German foreign minister (1966–69) and later as chancellor (1969–74), Willy Brandt undertook the historic mission of normalizing relations with the Soviet Union. Brandt began by accepting geopolitical realities in central Europe, including the existence of two German states. Without abandoning the long-term aspiration of reunification, Brandt believed that reducing tensions between East and West would lead to a gradual lowering of barriers between East and West Germany. For their part, the Soviets wanted recognition of their position in Eastern Europe and formal West German acceptance of the status quo.

Under Brandt's leadership the Federal Republic expanded trade with Eastern Europe and abandoned the Hallstein Doctrine (named for a previous foreign minister), which required the Federal Republic to sever relations with any nation (except the Soviet Union) that recognized the German Democratic Republic. In short order, Brandt established diplomatic relations with Yugoslavia and Romania. In 1970, he signed treaties with the Soviet Union and Poland providing for the mutual renunciation of force and the recognition that all borders in Europe, including the Oder–Neisse Line (dividing Germany and Poland) and the frontier between East and West Germany, were inviolable, thus confirming the division of Germany into two states and accepting the loss of German lands in the east to Poland and the Soviet Union. Significantly, the treaties recognized existing borders as inviolable rather than unalterable, thereby allowing for change by peaceful means. The normalization process continued in 1973 with a treaty between the Federal Republic and Czechoslovakia renouncing the 1938 Munich Agreement and all German claims to the Sudetenland.

West German ratification of the treaties was delayed pending completion of a four-power (United States, Great Britain, France, and the Soviet Union) agreement regulating the status of Berlin. The resulting Quadripartite Agreement, signed in September 1971, provided a legal basis for Western access to Berlin and ended the city's anomalous and vulnerable position. Anxious to ensure ratification of the Eastern Treaties, the Soviets acquiesced to Western demands that they, rather than the German Democratic Republic, guarantee access to Berlin and that West Berlin be allowed to have close political ties with the Federal Republic. In effect, the Soviets accepted the status quo in Berlin in exchange for Western acceptance of the status quo in Eastern Europe. The following year the Federal Republic and the German Democratic Republic concluded a Basic Treaty and other agreements that recognized each other's legitimacy and borders, renounced the use of force in relations between them, and provided for increased trade and travel between the two states.

The immediate results of Brandt's *Ostpolitik* included a major reduction in tension in central Europe, removal of Berlin as a chronic flashpoint, and increased East–West trade. Following the fall of communism in Eastern Europe some analysts argued that by accepting the status quo, *Ostpolitik* bolstered communist control and delayed communism's collapse. Other scholars contest this view and point out that the Soviets probably would not have accepted a peaceful end to their sphere of influence in Eastern Europe without the decade and a half of reduced tension that *Ostpolitik* fostered.

Meanwhile, Nixon and Kissinger had been working to improve US relations with the PRC. The Nixon administration had initiated contacts with the PRC shortly after taking office, but divisions within the Chinese leadership on the possibility and the value of improved relations with the United States had prevented progress. The May 1970 US invasion of Cambodia caused further delays, but in July 1971, Kissinger secretly traveled to the PRC to sound out Chinese leaders on the possibility of improved relations with the United States, and to lay to the groundwork for a visit to China by President Nixon.

To demonstrate its desire for improved relations, the United States raised only mild objections as the United Nations voted in September 1971 to admit the PRC and to award it China's seat on the Security Council, in the process expelling the Republic of China (Taiwan) from the organization. In addition, the United States "tilted" toward Pakistan in the December 1971 Indo-Pakistan War. Ignoring the war's regional roots, which involved India's support for the independence of East Pakistan, Nixon and Kissinger viewed it in global geopolitical terms as a conflict involving a Soviet client (India) bent on humiliating a US and Chinese ally (Pakistan), and by extension the United States and the PRC. Although the United States sent a naval task force into the Bay of Bengal to underline its support for its friend, this action did not affect the outcome of the war, which ended in Pakistan's defeat and the birth of the new nation of Bangladesh.

Nixon's visit to China in February 1972 put further pressure on the Soviets to head off a Sino-American strategic partnership. A public relations and a geopolitical success, the visit ended with a final communiqué that proclaimed Chinese and US opposition to Soviet "hegemony" in Asia. Although the communiqué noted their differing views on the future of Taiwan, it also pledged the United States to work toward a full normalization of relations with the PRC by 1976.

The US opening to China helped bring Soviet–American arms control negotiations, which had begun in late 1969, to a conclusion. The signing of the SALT I agreements in May 1972 during Nixon's visit to Moscow marked the high point of a short-lived period of limited détente, or relaxation of superpower tensions. The agreements curbed the destabilizing deployment of anti-ballistic missile (ABM) systems, set interim limits on offensive strategic nuclear weapons systems, and outlined a code of mutual restraint.

Although common sense might seem to suggest otherwise, ballistic missile defense systems were destabilizing because they could reduce an adversary's confidence in its ability to retaliate if attacked. This loss of confidence could increase incentives to strike first in a crisis. Analysts also feared that ABMs could stimulate the arms race if each side sought to overcome the other's defenses by deploying more missiles. To preserve each side's retaliatory capacity, the ABM treaty limited each side to the deployment of no more than 200 anti-ballistic missiles at two sites. (This was later reduced to 100 missiles at one site.) It also prohibited the development, testing, and deployment of ABM systems or components that were sea-based, air-based, space-based, or mobile land-based; put restrictions on the location of early warning radars and on upgrading missiles, launchers, or radar to give them ABM capability; and established a Standing Consultative Committee to deal with compliance issues. The treaty was of unlimited duration, though either side could withdraw on six months' notice.

An interim agreement of five years' duration set limits on ICBMs and submarine-launched ballistic missiles (SLBMs), essentially freezing the strategic arsenals of both sides at existing levels. When approved by the United States in October 1972, the interim agreement permitted the Soviet Union to deploy 1,618 ICBMs and 950 SLBM launchers while limiting the United States to 1,054 ICBMs and 656 SLBMs. The agreement allowed the Soviets more launchers because it excluded several areas where the United States had a large lead – strategic bombers, forward-based systems (US tactical and medium-range nuclear delivery systems in Europe and elsewhere that could strike Soviet territory) – and the national nuclear forces of the PRC, Great Britain, and France. The Soviets did not possess comparable capability due to reasons of geography and weaker allies. The United States was reluctant to include forward-based systems in the agreement for many reasons, including concerns about extended deterrence and alliance solidarity.

The interim agreement also did not address the issue of multiple independently targetable re-entry vehicles or MIRVs, multiple-missile warheads mounted on a single missile capable of being aimed at separate targets. MIRVs permitted the United States to increase the number of targets each missile could reach. The United States had begun deploying MIRVs in the early 1970s and did not want to give up this advantage. The Soviets lagged behind in this important new technology, and therefore insisted on higher ceilings for their launchers to offset the US advantage in MIRVs. Thus, while the interim agreement limited the United States to fewer ICBMs and SLBMs than were permitted for the Soviet Union, US missiles carried far more total warheads, approximately 4,800 to 2,000, due to MIRV technology.

MIRVs reduced the cost of expanding nuclear forces and had the potential to weaken mutual deterrence. The large number of warheads relative to launch vehicles rewarded offensive action by allowing an attacker to overwhelm its opponent's forces. In addition, a defender who relied on MIRVs would be at a disadvantage because of the reduced number of launch vehicles, and hence targets, an attacker would have to destroy. Another problem was that once the Soviets developed an MIRV capacity, which they did in the mid-1970s, their missiles, which tended to be larger than US missiles, could carry larger numbers of MIRVs and upset the strategic balance.

The Basic Principles Agreement that accompanied the SALT accords attempted to establish a set of guidelines for acceptable behavior that would minimize the likelihood of superpower confrontations. Both sides pledged to "do their utmost to avoid military confrontations and to prevent the outbreak of nuclear war," to exercise "restraint" in their mutual relations, and to "recognize that efforts to obtain unilateral advantage at the expense of the other, directly or indirectly, are inconsistent with these objectives." They also promised to renounce claims to special privileges in other regions.

The Soviets saw the Basic Principles Agreement as establishing a code of conduct for Soviet–American relations and as recognition of the Soviet Union as an equal superpower. Although interested in restraining Soviet behavior, Nixon and Kissinger viewed the agreements as a set of aspirations rather than as a binding code of conduct. They preferred to rely on linking progress in arms control and East–West trade with Soviet behavior in the Third World as a way to limit Soviet influence.

Satellite reconnaissance and electronic surveillance equipment enabled both sides to monitor compliance with the arms control agreements by technical means. This sidestepped the tricky issues of verification and inspection while allowing each side to have confidence that the other would not cheat. Compliance with the Basic Principles Agreement was much more difficult to monitor, however, since it involved qualitative rather than quantitative issues.

The Soviets regarded the possibility of increased trade with the United States as one of the potential benefits of improved relations with the United States. Following the Moscow summit, the Soviets made massive purchases of American grain, so much, in fact, that they drove up prices for US consumers. In October 1972, the Soviets agreed to repay over $700 million in lend–lease debts in exchange for a Nixon administration pledge to seek most favored nation trading status for the Soviet Union from Congress.

Although Soviet grain purchases became routine, Soviet–American trade was slow to develop. The United States viewed trade as an important bargaining lever to obtain concessions on political issues and was legally prohibited from selling the Soviets anything that could help them militarily. Trade with the Soviets was also unpopular while the Vietnam War was still going on. Finally, the ability to restrict trade became a means by which US critics of détente could express their displeasure with Soviet actions. In a series of amendments to trade legislation in 1973 and 1974, the US Congress blocked most favored nation trade status for the Soviet Union until the Soviets allowed increased emigration of Soviet

Jews, and set very low limits on the amount of trade credits the Soviets could receive from the US government.

Détente signified the mutual recognition by the primary protagonists in the Cold War that it was in their interests to regulate their relationship. Despite increased cooperation, especially in arms control, the Soviet–American relationship remained essentially competitive, however. Although détente in Europe continued to flourish, Soviet–American rivalry in the Third World interacted with continuing competition in the arms race to undermine the process.

5   From détente to confrontation, 1973–80

Following its high point in 1973, détente foundered as increased instability in the Third World and technological advances that threatened
mutual deterrence interacted to intensify Soviet–American distrust and
undercut political support for relaxed tensions between the two superpowers. During this period, the Third World experienced remarkable
turbulence, including several radical revolutions. Although deeply
rooted in indigenous developments and regional rivalries, instability in
the Third World created conditions that increased superpower rivalry.
Deteriorating relations in turn increased distrust and made arms control
agreements more difficult to reach.

In addition to these structural changes, the policies followed by the
United States and the Soviet Union also contributed to the demise of
détente. President Nixon's resignation due to the Watergate scandal
combined with disillusionment over the conduct of the Vietnam War to
undermine public support for an activist US world role. These same
factors also made Nixon's successor, Gerald R. Ford (1974–77), and
Secretary of State Henry Kissinger reluctant to appear "soft" on the
Soviets. Although often criticized for allegedly undermining pro-US
authoritarian regimes in the Third World, the human rights focus of
President Jimmy Carter's foreign policy (1977–81) provided a popular
rationale for renewed US involvement in the Third World and a more
confrontational relationship with the Soviet Union.

Soviet policies also contributed to the demise of détente. The determination of Soviet leader Leonid Brezhnev to match the US global
role led to high levels of military spending and increased involvement
in the Third World. These policies not only harmed relations with the
United States but undermined the long-term well-being of the Soviet
economy.

THIRD WORLD CONFLICT

During the 1970s, US officials often charged that the Soviet Union took advantage of détente to increase its influence in the Third World. The September 1973 military coup that overthrew the socialist government of President Salvador Allende Gossens of Chile raised questions, however, about US adherence to the pledge of mutual restraint made in the Basic Principles Agreement. Although Allende's fall was largely due to internal factors and scholars have yet to find evidence of direct US participation in the coup, the United States was deeply involved in efforts to undermine and overthrow Allende.

In the 1960s, the United States provided Chile with extensive economic assistance under the Alliance for Progress and covertly intervened in the 1964 presidential election to prevent an Allende victory. After Allende won a plurality in the 1970 presidential election, the Nixon administration, which viewed a freely elected Marxist government as a greater threat than Castro's Cuba, covertly financed a number of unsuccessful attempts to prevent him from taking office. During Allende's three years in office, the United States cut off economic assistance, opposed loans to Chile by international financial institutions, strengthened its ties to Chile's armed forces, and covertly financed numerous opposition groups. In short, US policies contributed substantially to the polarization of Chilean politics and to the weakening of Allende's government. Despite the brutality of the coup and its aftermath, which resulted in the death or disappearance of at least 3,000 Chileans, the United States welcomed the new government and quickly resumed economic assistance.

The Soviets had maintained their distance from Allende and had provided his government with only limited economic support. Nevertheless, they had hoped that détente would permit a peaceful road to socialism and regarded US actions in Chile as a betrayal of détente. Moreover, radical elements in the Soviet Union, the PRC, and elsewhere charged that the Soviet leadership was more interested in improving relations with the United States than in aiding progressive movements in the Third World. This criticism highlighted the dilemma détente presented to the Soviets: it could force them to choose between accommodation with the United States and support for their friends in the Third World.

The October 1973 Middle East War subjected détente to further stress as both superpowers took actions that appeared inconsistent with their commitment to relax tensions and to forego attempts to gain unilateral advantage. The war also underlined the danger of regional conflict drawing the superpowers into confrontation. Regional actors often had interests and ambitions that differed from those of their superpower patrons. In some cases, regional actors preferred superpower conflict to cooperation because it enhanced their ability to extract resources from the superpowers by portraying themselves as Cold War allies.

The war grew out of efforts by Egyptian leader Anwar Sadat to draw the superpowers into a settlement of the Arab–Israeli conflict, since Egypt and its allies were not strong enough on their own to defeat Israel. The Soviets had continued to supply arms to Egypt even after Sadat expelled Soviet advisers in 1972. Fearful of losing more influence in the Arab world, the Soviets had little leverage left to prevent Sadat and Syria from attacking Israel. After the war began, the Soviets supported Egypt and Syria by engaging in a massive resupply effort. Although the United States countered the Soviet effort by airlifting tons of weapons to Israel, the two superpowers were soon working together to stop the fighting. US aid enabled Israel to overcome early setbacks, and Israeli forces were soon on the verge of an overwhelming victory. The Soviets wanted to prevent a damaging defeat of their Arab allies and maintain their influence in the region. Although Henry Kissinger, who headed the US response, also wanted to avoid a crushing Arab defeat, he hoped to use the crisis as an opportunity to win over Sadat and increase US influence in the Middle East. A potentially serious situation arose when Brezhnev, in response to an Egyptian proposal that the United States and the Soviet Union send troops to the Middle East to enforce a cease-fire, warned that the Soviet Union might intervene on its own if the United States refused to participate. The United States responded by putting its nuclear forces on alert. According to recent research, the Soviets had no intention of sending troops, and the crisis ended when Israel halted its advance and began to observe a UN-sponsored cease-fire.[1]

Following the fighting, US diplomacy focused on excluding the Soviet Union from the peace settlement. After a brief and fruitless conference in Geneva that included the Soviets, Kissinger worked out the details of military disengagement and resolution of territorial disputes over a two-year period in a series of meetings with the leaders of Israel and the Arab states. Kissinger's efforts convinced Sadat that the United States was the key to a settlement and to turn to the Americans for economic and military assistance. In 1978, President Carter mediated a peace settlement between Egypt and Israel that provided for the return of the Sinai to Egypt and cemented the US–Egyptian alliance. The loss of Egypt, the most populous and militarily most powerful Arab state, was a serious blow to the Soviets in a region of great strategic importance.

The 1973 war led to an oil crisis in the West when the Arab members of OPEC (the Organization of Petroleum Exporting Countries) cut back production and embargoed shipments to the United States and The Netherlands in retaliation for their support of Israel.[2] The oil shortage soon ended, but oil prices quadrupled, contributing to inflation, economic stagnation, and high levels of unemployment. Although not directly related to the Cold War, the oil crisis evoked images of a weakened West. The United States was particularly affected because American popular culture tended to equate the private automobile and personal mobility with individual freedom. Moreover, the oil crisis coincided with increased competition from Western Europe and Japan and the decline of US heavy industry. Between 1970 and 1980, the US share of global output declined from around 38 percent to 25 percent. In the same period the share of the European Community rose from 26 to 30 percent and that of Japan from 8 to 10 percent.

In contrast, the Soviet Union, as an oil exporter, benefitted from higher oil prices. The Soviets were in the process of developing huge new oil and gas fields in Siberia, and higher prices increased their export earnings. While enabling the Soviet Union to import large amounts of Western grain and machinery, oil earnings also tended to mask increasingly severe economic problems and to reduce incentives for undertaking sorely needed structural reforms.

The fall of South Vietnam, Cambodia, and Laos to communist forces in the spring and summer of 1975 evoked even more powerful images of American decline. Following the withdrawal of US combat forces in early 1973, the United States continued to provide South Vietnam with economic and military assistance. In response to reports that the United States had been illegally conducting bombing operations in Cambodia the US Congress, in June 1973, cut off funding for US combat activities in or over North and South Vietnam, Cambodia, and Laos. Then, in November, Congress passed the War Powers Act which required the president to consult with Congress before committing US forces abroad.

The government of South Vietnam had become increasingly dependent on US support since its creation. Without US military power to protect it, US military and economic aid was not sufficient to ensure its survival. Following a brief offensive by communist forces, the government of South Vietnam collapsed in April 1975. Cambodia fell the same month to Pol Pot's Khmer Rouge, who were allied with the PRC rather than the Soviets. The communist Pathet Lao, who were backed by North Vietnam, took power in Laos in August.

At the same time that the wars in Southeast Asia were coming to an end, a conflict in Africa further undermined détente. In April 1974, a military coup ended forty years of authoritarian rule in Portugal. Radicalized by years of fighting "dirty" wars in defense of colonialism, Portugal's new military leaders quickly announced their intention to grant independence to Portugal's colonies. The impending end of Portuguese colonialism set off a civil war in Angola where three rival factions contended for power. Divided by regional and ethnic loyalties, the three groups also looked to different sources of external support. The National Front for the Liberation of Angola (FNLA), based in northeast Angola, received aid from the United States, the PRC, and Zaire (formerly known as the Congo). The Popular Movement for the Liberation of Angola (MPLA), which was strongest in the central part of the country, was backed by Cuba and the Soviet Union. The National Union for the Total Independence of Angola (UNITA), based in southern Angola, was supported by South Africa, which was concerned about developments on the border of Namibia (then known as South West Africa), which South Africa controlled.

Fighting broke out in February 1975. Even with covert assistance from the United States and the aid of combat troops from Zaire and South Africa, the FNLA and UNITA, despite working together, were unable to defeat the MPLA, which received timely assistance from Cuba and the Soviet Union. (The PRC pulled out of Angola in the summer of 1975 due to changes in its overall foreign policy and a desire not to be associated with South Africa.) The Cubans had been involved in aiding African liberation movements since the 1960s, and had responded to MPLA requests for assistance by sending around 500 military advisers to Angola in the fall of 1975. After South African forces invaded Angola in mid-October, Cuba, at first on its own and later with Soviet assistance, dispatched 11,000–12,000 combat troops to Angola. By mid-December, when the US Congress voted to cut off funding for the FNLA and UNITA, the Cuban forces had turned the tide.[3] Although the fighting continued, the Organization of African Unity and most African states officially recognized the MPLA as the government of Angola in February 1976.

Henry Kissinger feared that the Cuban presence in Angola could provide the Soviets with a base for the expansion of their influence in mineral-rich southern Africa. Similarly, President Carter's national security adviser, Zbigniew Brzezinski, warned that Soviet and Cuban involvement in the Horn of Africa, an area in the northeast corner of the continent close to the Middle East, could threaten Western access to Middle East oil. Although the turmoil in the Horn was deeply rooted in regional rivalries, the involvement of Soviet and Cuban troops in

Ethiopia led Brzezinski to view events there as part of a concerted Soviet offensive aimed at challenging US interests in the Persian Gulf and the Indian Ocean.

Soviet and Cuban involvement in the Horn of Africa grew out of a dispute between Ethiopia and Somalia over the Ogaden, a sparsely populated, largely desert region in Ethiopia inhabited mainly by ethnic Somalis. The United States had established an intelligence listening post in Ethiopia in 1953, and had provided the country with economic and military assistance. After a military coup removed aging emperor Haile Selassie in 1974, US relations with Ethiopia began to deteriorate. The United States cut off aid to Ethiopia in 1977 in response to an arms deal between Ethiopia and the Soviet Union. (Meanwhile, technical advances had made the intelligence post obsolete.) The Soviets had been providing aid to Somalia since the 1960s in return for use of the port of Berbera to support their naval presence in the Indian Ocean.

The Somalis were not pleased with growing Soviet aid to Ethiopia, and turned to the United States for help. After receiving assurances that the United States would help them obtain defensive weapons, Somali forces invaded the Ogaden in July 1977. The Ethiopian government, faced with rising domestic discontent due to its repressive policies and a major insurgency in its northern province of Eritrea (a former Italian colony annexed by Ethiopia after World War II), called on the Soviet Union for help. After an unsuccessful attempt to mediate the dispute, the Soviets, in November, sent military equipment and Soviet military advisers, and airlifted some 12,000–17,000 Cuban combat troops to Ethiopia. With this assistance the Ethiopians routed the Somalis and regained control of the Ogaden. Although they refused to support an invasion of Somalia, the Soviets helped the Ethiopian government regain control of Eritrea, where all of Ethiopia's ports were located. (The Cubans had earlier aided the Eritrean rebels and refused to fight in Eritrea.) In 1980, Somalia, which had ejected the Soviets from Berbera, granted the United States access to its ports in return for US military assistance. In effect, the United States and the Soviet Union had swapped clients, but some US observers viewed the developments as a Western defeat.

EUROPEAN DÉTENTE

In contrast to relations in the Third World, détente in Europe continued to make progress. In August 1975, two years of negotiations under the auspices of the Conference on Security and Cooperation in Europe

(CSCE) culminated in a compromise agreement that balanced Soviet desires to legitimate existing European boundaries with Western concerns to promote liberalization in Eastern Europe and to preserve the possibility of peaceful change. Known as the Helsinki Accords after the city in which negotiations took place, the final act consisted of three sets or "baskets" of agreements. Basket One dealt with security issues and included declarations on the importance of sovereignty and self-determination, the non-use of force, the inviolability of frontiers, the principle of non-intervention in internal affairs, and respect for human rights and fundamental freedoms. This first basket also included a number of confidence-building measures, such as advance notification of large-scale military maneuvers, designed to reduce tension. Basket Two outlined ways to increase East–West cooperation in economics, science and technology, and the environment, as well as trade. Basket Three dealt with humanitarian cooperation and contained provisions relating to the free flow of people, information, and ideas.

Although some critics complained that the Helsinki agreements legitimized the boundary changes imposed on Eastern Europe by the Soviets after World War II, the agreements merely recognized reality. In addition, as in the earlier West German treaties with the Soviet Union, Poland, and Czechoslovakia, existing boundaries were recognized as inviolable rather than as permanent, which did not rule out peaceful change. Moreover, the human rights provisions of Basket Three provided human rights activists throughout Europe, but especially in Eastern Europe and the Soviet Union, with international approval of their efforts. As in the case of *Ostpolitik*, the human rights and economic provisions of the Helsinki agreements probably played a positive role in breaking down the barriers that divided Europe.

While European détente continued to flourish, especially in the area of East–West trade, the Soviet deployment of a new intermediate-range mobile missile raised the chronic issue of the US commitment to European security. In 1977, the Soviets began deploying SS-20 intermediate-range missiles, an advanced mobile missile capable of carrying three independently targetable warheads. The Soviets regarded the SS-20 as a replacement for older, less capable systems and as a necessary counter to US forward-based systems and the national nuclear forces of Britain and France. Western analysts, in contrast, warned that the SS-20 could give the Soviets regional nuclear superiority, allowing them to wage and win a nuclear war in Europe while Soviet ICBMs deterred a US strategic response. This would sever the link between US and West European security, already threatened by US–Soviet strategic parity, and leave Western Europe open to Soviet political pressure.

The Soviet decision to deploy the SS-20s proved counterproductive as NATO accelerated existing plans for the deployment in Western Europe of US Pershing II intermediate-range ballistic missiles and Tomahawk ground-launched cruise missiles (highly accurate, low-flying, subsonic missiles that could evade an adversary's radar). These highly accurate systems were capable of reaching targets within Soviet territory, and the short amount of time it would take for a Pershing II to strike targets in the Soviet Union greatly reduced warning times. The Soviets complained that deployment of these missiles would greatly increase tensions and the risk of nuclear war and offered to negotiate the issue, provided that NATO refrained from deploying the US missiles. NATO, however, decided on December 12, 1979 to proceed with the planned deployment of almost 600 Pershing II and Tomahawk missiles, which was scheduled to begin in 1983, while at the same time offering to begin talks with the Soviets on limiting theater nuclear weapons. By the time NATO reached its decision, however, the overall future of arms control, and of détente, was in doubt.

ARMS CONTROL

The SALT I agreements had held out the promise of an end to the arms race. With the ABM Treaty sharply limiting defensive systems, and thus depriving both sides of the ability to defend themselves against a nuclear attack, a fairly small number of offensive weapons should have been sufficient to ensure mutual deterrence, which was based on each side being able to retaliate effectively after absorbing an attack.

This opportunity was lost for several reasons. First, technological change, especially improved accuracy and the greater number of warheads due to MIRVs, vastly increased both sides' chances of being able to destroy the other side's strategic forces, or at least its ICBMs, and hence its ability to retaliate following an attack. This emerging counter-force capability held out the possibility (and temptation) of a successful first strike, and thus undermined mutual deterrence.[4]

In addition, the very different structures of the US and Soviet nuclear forces made comparison difficult and exacerbated the problems raised by the emerging counterforce capabilities. The US force structure was based on the concept of a strategic triad, a more or less balanced force of ICBMs, submarine-launched ballistic missiles (SLBMs), and manned strategic bombers. In contrast, the Soviets lacked forward bases and their SLBMs were far less capable than their US counterparts, so they relied much more heavily on land-based ICBMs. In addition,

Soviet missiles tended to be larger than comparable US missiles because the Soviets lagged behind in miniaturization technology and their guidance systems were less accurate. Due to the different force structures, each side sought different solutions to the core problem of mutual deterrence – ensuring the ability to retaliate against an adversary's attack. Whereas the United States relied heavily on the survivability of its SLBM force to provide an effective deterrent against a Soviet attack, Soviet defense planners looked to large numbers of ICBMs in order to be sure of their ability to retaliate against a US attack.

Technological change also increased the problem of verification. Whereas existing satellite and radar systems were adequate to verify quantitative issues like the number of missile launchers or strategic bombers, it was much more difficult to assess such qualitative issues as throw-weight (the number and power of warheads a missile could carry), the number of MIRVed warheads on any particular missile, or the effective range of bombers and cruise missiles. Due to their small size, cruise missiles were easy to hide and thus presented serious verification problems.

Another problem was that the United States continued to insist that the SALT process applied only to the central strategic systems of the two superpowers. This definition excluded US forward-based systems as well as the national nuclear forces of Great Britain, France, and the PRC, even though all were capable of destroying targets on Soviet soil. Unlike the West, the Soviets possessed no allies with nuclear forces targeted on the United States. Reductions in the central systems of the two superpowers made such shorter-range forces more important in the overall strategic balance.

Finally, the US strategy of extended deterrence was predicated on overall US strategic superiority. According to this view, the function of US strategic forces was not only to deter a Soviet attack on the United States but to deter possible Soviet advances elsewhere in the world. Overall strategic superiority was needed to compensate for assumed Soviet conventional superiority in Europe and to discourage Soviet "adventurism" in the Third World. Parity would not be enough to maintain extended deterrence because it would result in mutual deterrence at the global level and thus greater freedom for the Soviets on the regional level, especially in Europe. Soviet strategic superiority would not only erode extended deterrence but would also put the United States itself at risk of a Soviet pre-emptive strike.

These problems made the process of moving beyond the SALT I interim agreement very difficult. Nevertheless, the United States and the

Soviet Union were able to agree on the broad outlines of a SALT II agreement at a meeting in Vladivostok in November 1974 between Brezhnev and President Gerald R. Ford, who had assumed office in August 1974 following Nixon's resignation due to the Watergate scandal. Senate dissatisfaction with the unequal launcher totals in the SALT I interim agreement had resulted in a non-binding but politically important resolution that stipulated that all future arms control agreements insist on equal aggregate numbers of missile launchers. Accordingly, the Vladivostok accord set equal aggregate levels of 2,400 missile launchers and strategic bombers with a sub-limit of 1,320 launchers with MIRV capability. It left unresolved the issues of cruise missiles (where the United States enjoyed a large lead), a new Soviet bomber (the "Backfire"), which the United States claimed had strategic capability, and US forward-based systems and the national nuclear forces of Great Britain, France, and the PRC.

Critics of arms control, led by Senator Henry Jackson, charged that the Vladivostok agreement set too high a limit on the number of launchers and did not limit Soviet "heavy" missiles. As noted earlier, Soviet missiles tended to be larger than comparable US missiles due to deficiencies in accuracy and miniaturization, which was essential to MIRVs. Once the Soviets began to improve the accuracy of their missiles and to master MIRV technology, their larger or "heavy" missiles could carry a greater number of larger warheads. This advantage in throw-weight could eventually give the Soviets the theoretical capacity to launch a pre-emptive strike against the US land-based ICBM force, and still retain plenty of warheads in reserve for another attack if the United States decided to retaliate. Armed with this advantage the Soviets might be tempted to launch a counterforce attack on the United States on the assumption that, faced with the unpalatable option of mutual destruction, the United States would surrender. At the least, the strategic superiority conveyed by the advantage in throw-weight could greatly increase the Soviet Union's freedom of action and inhibit the United States from countering Soviet advances. In a circular argument, Jackson and his allies maintained that Soviet activism in the Third World confirmed their claim that the growth and development of the Soviet nuclear arsenal had put the Soviets ahead in the arms race.

This "nightmare scenario" ignored several important constraints. First, it assumed that the Soviet missiles would function with a high degree of accuracy although no one had tested ICBMs over the magnetic North Pole, the route that US and Soviet ICBMs would have to follow. Second, it ignored the other two legs of the US strategic triad, SLBMs and manned bombers, as well as US forward-based systems in

Europe and elsewhere. It also overlooked the fact that a Soviet counter-force strike would result in millions of civilian deaths and would probably create irresistible pressure for retaliation. Finally, it assumed that the Soviet leadership would be willing to risk the nuclear destruction of their homeland for political gains.

The critics of arms control were too strong politically to ignore, however. In an effort to address their concerns, the Carter administration, shortly after taking office, proposed a new SALT II agreement that called for lower ceilings on the number of launchers allowed each side and deep cuts in the number of Soviet heavy missiles. In addition, the Soviets would have to agree not to convert the Backfire bomber into a full-fledged strategic bomber. As compensation, the United States agreed to ban any new ICBMs, which would halt development of the MX missile, a large, mobile ICBM that could carry a large number of MIRVs. (An additional US offer to put a 2,500-kilometer limit on the range of cruise missiles was meaningless since no existing cruise missiles were capable of flying so far.)

Heavily committed to the Vladivostok agreement, the Soviets immediately rejected the US proposal, which had been accompanied by public criticism of Soviet human rights policies. Following this setback, it took two more years of negotiations before the two nations were able to reach agreement. In the meantime, the Carter administration sought to put pressure on the Soviet Union by playing the "China card." Although initially conceived as a form of triangular diplomacy whereby the United States would balance its relations with the Soviet Union and the PRC in order to influence both, the US opening to China had quickly become an effort to enlist the PRC in a strategic partnership against the Soviet Union.[5] The PRC had resisted, however, and in mid-1974 moved toward a policy of independence from both superpowers. In the spring of 1978, Carter's national security adviser Zbigniew Brzezinski renewed efforts to develop a de facto alliance with the PRC against the Soviet Union.

By this time, Chinese policy had shifted again, and the PRC's leaders wanted US help in blocking Soviet influence in Asia. They insisted, however, that the United States end its ties with Taiwan. Negotiations during the summer and fall of 1978 led to a compromise whereby the United States reaffirmed its adherence to the principle that Taiwan was part of China. The United States agreed to recognize the PRC as the sole government of China, to terminate its diplomatic relations and its mutual defense treaty with the Republic of China, and to withdraw US troops from Taiwan. The United States insisted, however, on the right to continue trade and cultural relations with Taiwan and to continue to sell

Taiwan defensive weapons. The PRC stopped short of pledging not to use force against Taiwan, agreeing only not to contradict the US expectation that the ultimate status of Taiwan would be settled by peaceful means. In mid-December, the United States and the PRC announced that full diplomatic relations would begin on January 1, 1979. In celebration of their renewed ties, Chinese leader Deng Xiaoping visited the United States in late January 1979.

Playing the "China card" not only soured relations with the Soviets, it sidetracked efforts to normalize relations with Vietnam. Normalization talks had begun in the spring of 1977, but quickly became deadlocked when the Vietnamese demanded that the United States provide $3.25 billion in economic assistance promised by President Nixon in early 1973. The United States maintained that whatever Nixon had promised, any obligation to provide aid had been nullified by the North Vietnamese conquest of South Vietnam. US intransigence on the issue led the Vietnamese to drop their demand for aid, but deteriorating relations between Vietnam and Cambodia prevented a settlement. The United States viewed the conflict between Vietnam and Cambodia in geopolitical terms as one between the PRC and the Soviet Union, and, ignoring the genocidal nature of the Pol Pot regime, sided with Cambodia. Not surprisingly, Vietnam moved closer to the Soviet Union, signing a treaty of friendship and cooperation in November 1978. In exchange for military and economic assistance, Vietnam agreed to allow regular Soviet use of the former US bases at Cam Rahn Bay and Danang. A month later, Vietnamese forces invaded Cambodia, defeated the Pol Pot regime, and installed a friendly government. During his visit to the United States, Deng Xiaoping had informed his hosts that the PRC would punish Vietnam for its attack on Cambodia. The following month, Chinese forces mounted a brief invasion of Vietnam.[6]

Due to these distractions, and to the complexity of the issues, completion of the arms control negotiations was delayed until June 1979, when Carter and Brezhnev signed the SALT II treaty at a summit in Vienna. Described by one scholar as "too detailed and too technical to be understood fully by the average citizen, or, for that matter, by the average senator," SALT II balanced the Soviet advantage in heavy missiles and throw-weight with US advantages in the total number of warheads, SLBMs, cruise missiles, and the forward-based systems that remained outside of the SALT process.[7]

The treaty limited each side to 2,400 strategic launch vehicles until the end of 1981, and to 2,250 from then until the expiration of the treaty at the end of 1985. Within the overall limits, sub-ceilings limited each side to 1,320 MIRVed missiles and heavy bombers equipped with long-range cruise missiles, 1,200 MIRVed land-based missiles and SLBMs, and 820 MIRVed land-based missiles. In addition to these numerical limits, the treaty restricted the Soviets to their existing total of 308 heavy missiles, limited the number of warheads that could be placed on various types of missiles, limited each side to testing and deploying one new ICBM system, and specified various measures to facilitate verification. A separate protocol banned the deployment (but not testing) of ground- and sea-launched cruise missiles with ranges of more than 600 kilometers, and a letter from Brezhnev to Carter gave assurances that the Backfire would not be converted into a strategic bomber. Finally, the treaty committed the two sides to begin work immediately on a SALT III agreement that would contain significant cuts in the arsenals of both sides.

Hearings during the summer of 1979 revealed strong opposition to the treaty. Although some of the criticism was based on the treaty's provisions, the larger problem was continued instability and conflict in the Third World and the resulting damage to US–Soviet relations.

CONTINUED CONFLICT IN THE THIRD WORLD

In January 1979, the shah of Iran, an American ally since World War II, fled his country in the face of a massive popular uprising. Following the overthrow of Musaddiq in 1953, US economic, military, and security assistance had helped the shah establish a royal dictatorship. He lacked legitimacy, however, because his father had seized power in the 1920s with British support and because his power was dependent on the support he received from the United States. As oil revenues skyrocketed in the 1970s, so did discontent with the shah's rule. He squandered much of the money on weapons and prestige projects, and his autocratic efforts to force the Westernization of Iran resulted in increasing inequality, widespread corruption, and the alienation of much of Iranian society. As oil prices fell in the second half of the 1970s, rising discontent, channeled and led by influential religious leaders, erupted into open revolt early in 1978. Gradually but steadily increasing in strength, the opposition eventually overwhelmed efforts by the shah's army and secret police to contain it. Losing confidence in the loyalty of his security forces and seriously ill, the shah rejected US suggestions that he use force to crush the revolt and instead fled the country in January 1979.

The fall of the shah was a serious setback to the US position in the Middle East. Since the 1940s, the United States had viewed a pro-Western and stable Iran as essential to containing Soviet expansion in the Middle East and maintaining Western access to the region's oil. Identifying the shah and the monarchy with Western economic and strategic interests in Iran, the United States had supported him against internal as well as external opponents. The Nixon Doctrine had enhanced the shah's regional role as the United States looked to Iran as one of the pillars of pro-Western stability in the Persian Gulf, and rewarded the shah with almost unlimited access to the latest US military equipment.

The revolution against the shah caught the United States by surprise, and it took the US leaders a long time to realize the seriousness of the situation. In addition, the absence of Soviet involvement made it difficult for the United States to develop a coherent response. As it gradually became clear that the shah could not be saved, the United States was unable to identify an acceptable alternative and was forced to let events take their course. In February 1979, the leader of the Islamic opposition, Ayatollah Rouhallah Khomeini, returned to Iran from exile and quickly emerged as the effective leader of Iran, though he had no formal governmental position.

The United States was already unpopular in Iran due to its long support for the shah, and its efforts to maintain influence there by bolstering pro-American groups became entangled in the internal struggle for power and probably enhanced anti-American sentiment. After the Carter administration allowed the shah to enter the United States for medical treatment, a group of Khomeini supporters seized the American embassy in Tehran in November 1979 and held fifty-three Americans hostage for over a year. In addition, the Iranian revolution had disrupted world oil markets and led to a tripling of oil prices. (Higher oil prices also played a role in the origins of the Third World debt crisis that emerged in the 1980s as banks recycled oil revenues, petrodollars, to developing countries.) Although Iran was also anti-Soviet, the Iranian revolution and the subsequent hostage crisis were widely viewed as further evidence of the decline of American power.

In July 1979, another long-standing US ally, Anastasio Somoza Debayle of Nicaragua, was overthrown in a violent popular revolution. The Somoza family had ruled Nicaragua since the 1930s, their power based on control of the US-trained and armed National Guard. By the late 1970s, rising popular discontent, led by the Frente Sandinista de Liberación Nacional (FSLN or Sandinistas), but including a wide range of groups across Nicaraguan society, threatened Somoza's hold on power. In addition, Somoza's repressive rule had become an embarrassment for the Carter administration's human rights policies, and such regional allies as Costa Rica, Panama, and Venezuela were calling for his removal. Although concerned about the FSLN's Marxist–Leninist origins and ties to Cuba, the United States was unable to find an acceptable alternative. In June 1979, the Organization of American States rebuffed a US attempt to head off a Sandinista military victory by inserting an OAS peacekeeping force. By the time Somoza finally left Nicaragua in mid-July almost 50,000 Nicaraguans had died, the economy was in ruins, and the national treasury was empty.

The Soviet Union was not involved in the Nicaraguan revolution, and Cuba played only a limited role advising and supplying the Sandinistas. Nevertheless, conservative groups in the United States viewed the Sandinista victory as one for communism and a threat to US security. The "discovery" of a Soviet combat brigade in Cuba by US intelligence in the summer of 1979 further increased fears of a growing Soviet threat to US interests in Latin America. Subsequent analysis revealed that the brigade (around 2,000–3,000 troops) had been in Cuba since the early 1960s, but the furor created by the issue further damaged détente.

A coup by reformist military officers in El Salvador in October 1979 underlined the fragility of pro-US authoritarian regimes in Central America. A small, densely populated country, El Salvador had a long history of repressive rule by a narrow oligarchy allied with the military. A broad spectrum of opposition groups emerged in the 1970s following a decade of mounting tensions due to the expansion of export agriculture at the expense of peasant farmers. Foreclosing the possibility of peaceful change within the political system, the military manipulated elections and supported death squads, financed by the oligarchy, to eliminate their opponents.

The new government initially hoped to forestall revolution by reaching out to popular organizations and implementing long-needed reforms. Senior officers quickly regained control, however, and death-squad activity increased, soon reaching the level of 1,000 murders a month. Any reform impulse atrophied. In response, several leftist opposition groups joined in an umbrella organization, named the Frente Farabundo Martí de Liberación Nacional (FMLN) after the leader of a 1932 peasant uprising. Composed of military and civilian wings, the FMLN gained support rapidly.

The Soviet occupation of Afghanistan at the end of December 1979, along with the US response, finished détente and marked the beginning of a brief but intense period of Soviet–American confrontation. The Soviet Union, like Tsarist Russia, had a long-standing interest in Afghanistan, but had been content to tolerate an independent and non-aligned Afghanistan as a buffer on its southern flank. In April 1978, the pro-Soviet People's Democratic Party of Afghanistan (PDPA) overthrew the government in a violent coup. Although the Soviets were probably not involved in the coup, which arose out of internal and regional rivalries, they welcomed the new government, responded favorably to its requests for economic and military assistance, and signed a treaty of friendship and cooperation in December 1978. The new government's attempts to push through a program of radical social and economic reform ran into stiff resistance, especially in the conservative countryside, and armed resistance soon developed. The Soviets, in addition to sending military advisers and increasing amounts of military assistance, attempted to convince the government to moderate its policies. Divisions in the PDPA thwarted its efforts. Soviet attempts to remove Hafizullah Amin, leader of one of the factions, whom the Soviets saw as the chief obstacle to changing policy, backfired and resulted in an increase in Amin's power.

By late 1979, the opposition, which was receiving aid from the PRC, Pakistan, and possibly the United States, was in control of most of the countryside. The Soviets feared that an opposition victory could result in a radical Islamic regime taking power, increasing Iran's influence in the region and possibly causing unrest in the Soviet Union's Central Asian republics. Another concern was that Amin, who had initiated contacts with US intelligence, might "pull a Sadat" and move Afghanistan into the American camp in order to preserve his personal power. Not only would this be a tremendous blow to Soviet prestige, but it could result, in the worst case, in the deployment of American missiles in Afghanistan that could reach targets in Central Asia and Siberia.[8]

With détente already in deep trouble, the Soviets decided that the least damaging course was to send troops to Afghanistan, replace Amin with a government that would heed their advice, and try to contain the resistance, while gradually winning back the support of the population with a more moderate program of economic and social reform. On December 25, 1979, several thousand Soviet troops poured across the border between the two countries while Soviet special forces, airlifted to Kabul, Afghanistan's capital, killed Amin and several of his associates, and installed a new government under a rival Afghan communist. Although sufficient to prevent the collapse of the Afghan government, the Soviet forces, which soon numbered over 100,000, were not enough to defeat the opposition, which retreated to the countryside and waged a guerrilla war.

The Carter administration responded by curtailing trade with the Soviet Union, urging a Western boycott of the 1980 Summer Olympics to be held in Moscow, increasing military spending, and withdrawing the SALT II treaty from Senate consideration. The United States, along with the PRC, Pakistan, Egypt, and Saudi Arabia also channeled increasing amounts of assistance to the Afghan resistance, known as the mujahedin, who harassed the Soviet occupation forces for the next nine years.

The Soviets viewed their intervention in Afghanistan as a defensive move to prevent the humiliating defeat of an ally and the emergence of a hostile regime on their border. The United States, in contrast, saw the Soviet action as the culmination of a Soviet geopolitical offensive initiated under the cover of détente. Specifically, the United States interpreted the Soviet occupation as part of an offensive plan to dominate the Persian Gulf region and deny its oil to the West. Although Afghanistan's landlocked location and rugged mountainous terrain made it an unlikely route to the Persian Gulf, the Iranian revolution and earlier Soviet involvement in the Horn of Africa had made the United States extremely sensitive to threats to Western access to Middle East oil.

In January 1980, President Carter announced that "any attempt by any outside force to gain control of the Persian Gulf region will be regarded as an assault on the vital interests of the United States of America, and such an assault will be repelled by any means necessary, including military force." To back up his statement, which was purposively patterned on the Truman Doctrine, Carter accelerated planning, under way since the fall of the shah, for the creation of a Rapid Deployment Force that would enable the United States to react quickly to crises in the region.

Carter also moved to strengthen US military power. In July 1980, he approved Presidential Directive 59, which placed greater emphasis on counterforce targeting doctrine and authorized a massive increase in military spending. In combination with the earlier US decision to deploy the MX missile and NATO's December 1979 decision to deploy highly accurate IRBMs and cruise missiles in Europe, PD-59 appeared to the Soviets as a rejection of mutual deterrence, the very foundation of détente. In addition, the United States sought to put further pressure on the Soviets by tightening its strategic partnership with the PRC, permitting the Chinese access to advanced military equipment and technology previously denied them. The United States also granted the PRC most favored nation trade status, a privilege still denied the Soviet Union.

The demise of détente demonstrated the close and mutually reinforcing relationship between arms control and overall Soviet–American relations. Improved relations in the early 1970s had provided an environment in which arms control could proceed successfully, while arms control agreements symbolized and strengthened improved relations. As Soviet–American relations deteriorated due to instability in the Third World, arms control also suffered. In addition, continued competition in the arms race contributed to mutual mistrust by raising concerns that the "other side" was taking advantage of détente to gain unilateral advantage in the Cold War.

6 The rise and fall of the second Cold War, 1981–91

Carter's successor, Ronald Reagan (1981–89), denounced the Soviet Union as an immoral "evil empire," and fought the last phase of the Cold War vigorously on all fronts. Alleging that the Soviets were the source of most of the world's problems, Reagan persuaded the US Congress to approve massive increases in military spending, effectively ended arms control negotiations with the Soviets, and pursued an aggressive policy to roll back Soviet influence in the Third World. Reagan's policies resulted in a mushrooming budget deficit; a powerful, and at times anti-US, peace movement in Western Europe; strains within the NATO alliance; and a heightening of Cold War tensions.

This "second Cold War" proved short-lived, however. After Mikhail Gorbachev came to power in 1985, the Soviet Union began to pursue policies aimed at improving relations with the United States. With the Soviets making most of the concessions, the United States and the Soviet Union reached important arms control agreements. In 1989, faced with chronic unrest in Eastern Europe and economic decline at home, the Soviets allowed communist regimes in Eastern Europe to collapse. The following year, they agreed to German reunification on Western terms. Improved East–West relations and the Soviet Union's retreat from a world role also led to the withdrawal of Soviet troops from Afghanistan in early 1989 and facilitated negotiated settlements to local and regional conflicts in southern Africa, Southeast Asia, and Central America.

THE NEW COLD WAR

During the Reagan administration (1981–89), the United States intensified the military build-up begun during the last years of the Carter administration and spent over $2 trillion to build up US conventional and nuclear forces. Reagan revived the B-1 bomber program that Carter had shelved, continued development of the B-2 (Stealth) bomber, and accelerated deployment of the MX ICBM and the Trident submarine missile system (very accurate missile systems with MIRV capabilities). Much of the increased expenditure focused on conventional forces, including an expansion of the navy from 450 to 600 ships. The Reagan administration also expanded US covert action and increased US military assistance to pro-US governments and groups, including anti-communist insurgents in Afghanistan, Angola, Cambodia, and Nicaragua.

A key element in the build-up was the Strategic Defense Initiative (SDI), announced by Reagan in March 1983. SDI was a technologically ambitious and extremely expensive plan to develop a nationwide ballistic-missile defense system that would deploy weapons in outer space to destroy enemy missiles in flight. Popularly known as Star Wars, SDI threatened to violate several US–Soviet agreements, including the Limited Test Ban Treaty of 1963, the Outer Space Treaty of 1967, and the ABM Treaty of 1972. Although research on defensive systems might be permissible under the ABM Treaty, it specifically included provisions that required each side not to develop, test, or deploy ABM systems or components that were "sea-based, air-based, space-based, or mobile land-based."[1]

Many analysts regarded SDI as a dangerous and destabilizing attack on mutual deterrence, which was based on each side's ability to retaliate against a nuclear attack. They pointed out that while it was highly unlikely that the United States would be able to develop a system that would be effective against the full force of a first strike, it might be possible to develop a system that would be effective against the few remaining forces the Soviet Union would have left to retaliate against a US first strike. Thus SDI had the potential to give the United States the capacity and confidence to launch a pre-emptive first strike.

Whatever US intentions, many analysts also warned that SDI would accelerate the arms race. The most likely Soviet response would be to increase the numbers of their missiles in order to overwhelm US defenses. In contrast to hopes that SDI would force the Soviets to increase military expenditure beyond what they could afford, such a response would cost far less than the requisite US countervailing defensive systems.

In addition to re-establishing US military superiority, which they believed had been lost during détente, and regaining the initiative in the Cold War, Reagan and some of his supporters later claimed that they planned to use an arms race, especially in fields where the United States was technologically superior, to place great strain on the Soviet economy. Although the US build-up, and especially SDI, alarmed the Soviets, there is no evidence that Soviet defense spending, which had begun to level off in the mid-1970s, increased significantly in response to Reagan's initiatives.

Whether or not the US build-up contributed to the collapse of the Soviet Union, the rise in military expenditures coupled with tax cuts created a mushrooming US budget deficit. The national debt rose from $1 trillion in 1980 to $2.5 trillion in 1988. Although increased spending and the tax cuts stimulated the economy, increased government borrowing to finance the budget deficits helped keep interest rates high, which attracted foreign capital and drove up the value of the dollar. This, in turn, made US exports more expensive and imports cheaper, and contributed to a skyrocketing trade deficit. By 1986, the United States was the world's largest debtor.

The US military build-up was part of an overall strategy of increasing US strength before engaging in arms control negotiations with the Soviet Union. In the deadlocked negotiations on the issue of intermediate-range nuclear forces in Europe, the Reagan administration put forth what became known as the "zero option:" the United States offered to cancel plans to deploy Pershing II IRBMs and Tomahawk cruise missiles in exchange for the Soviets dismantling all their intermediate-range missiles in Europe and elsewhere. Not surprisingly, the Soviets rejected the US proposal since it would require them to eliminate not only the recently deployed SS-20s but other missiles that had been deployed for as long as twenty years while leaving in place air- and sea-based US forward-based systems and the national nuclear forces of Great Britain and France.

There is evidence that the United States put forth the zero option in the expectation that the Soviets would reject it, thus clearing the way for the deployment of the Pershing II and Tomahawk missiles. Whatever the US intent, it is clear that the US and Soviet positions were irreconcilable. The main reason NATO had proposed the INF deployment was to ensure the coupling of US conventional and tactical nuclear forces in Europe with US intercontinental nuclear forces. In contrast, the Soviets wanted to head off the deployments because they significantly augmented the US ability to strike targets in the Soviet Union.[2] Thus, although negotiations continued, no compromise was possible. In the fall of 1983, NATO began deploying the missiles. In response, the Soviets terminated the INF talks without agreeing to a date for their resumption.

A similar process played out in regard to negotiations regarding strategic weapons. Although opposed to the SALT II treaty, the Reagan administration decided in late 1981 to observe its provisions as long as the Soviets did likewise. In the meantime, the United States and the Soviet Union began new talks to reduce strategic weapons. The initial US proposal in the new negotiations, renamed Strategic Arms Reduction Talks (START), called for deep cuts in total nuclear weapons and seemed designed to be rejected. Although overall levels would nominally be equal, the details of the US plan required deep cuts in the Soviet Union's land-based missiles, the heart of its arsenal, while allowing the United States to proceed with the planned modernization of all parts of its strategic triad. The Soviets rejected the US proposal and the talks remained deadlocked until the Soviets canceled them in November 1983 at the same time as they walked out of the INF talks.

Reagan and his supporters blamed the Soviet Union for instability in the Third World and followed a confrontational policy toward Third World regimes they deemed hostile. The United States also provided increased military and other assistance to pro-US Third World regimes, including many regimes with deplorable human rights records. In addition to trying to reduce Soviet influence in the Third World, the Reagan administration moved aggressively to reduce government involvement in Third World economies.

The initial focus of US policy toward the Third World during the Reagan administration was El Salvador. In March 1980, a right-wing death squad had murdered Archbishop Oscar Romero as he was saying mass. Then, in December 1980, the Carter administration had suspended military aid to El Salvador following the rape and murder of four American churchwomen by government troops. Meanwhile, leftist guerrilla forces, encouraged by growing popular support, decided to launch a "final offensive" in January 1981 to overthrow the government before the Reagan administration took office. The guerrilla offensive received some support from the Soviet Union and Cuba. In addition to their belief that "progressive revolutions were morally right and historically inevitable," Soviet leaders might have aided the Salvadoran guerrillas in retaliation for US support of the Afghan resistance.[3] The offensive failed, in part because the Carter administration, fearing a guerrilla victory, resumed military aid to the Salvadoran government.

Ignoring the internal causes of the civil war, the Reagan administration focused on the support the Salvadoran guerrillas received from the Soviet Union, Cuba, and Nicaragua. Secretary of State Alexander Haig wanted to "go to the source," and blockade Cuba, but the United States settled for a massive increase in military and economic assistance to El Salvador. In addition to military aid, the United States organized, financed, and supervised elections in 1982; pressured the Salvadoran government to implement a limited land reform; and tried to convince the Salvadoran military to stop supporting death squads. Little changed, however, and the guerrillas continued to gain ground. In 1984, after centrist Christian Democrat José Napoleón Duarte won the presidency with massive US support, the United States further increased its aid to El Salvador. In the absence of any meaningful reforms, even a vastly increased military effort, while preventing a rebel victory, was unable to defeat the guerrillas and bring the civil war to an end.

By this time, the Reagan administration's focus had shifted to Nicaragua. Some of the Soviet and Cuban aid to the Salvadoran guerrillas had passed through Nicaragua. In April 1981, the United States suspended economic assistance to Nicaragua. A month earlier, President Reagan had authorized the Central Intelligence Agency to support covert activity in Central America to stop arms shipments to guerrilla movements. By the end of the year, the CIA was organizing and supporting a military force of Nicaraguan exiles, composed largely but not exclusively of former members of Somoza's National Guard. Although the original mission of this force, known as *contrarevolucionarios* or Contras, was to prevent arms shipments from Nicaragua reaching the Salvadoran guerrillas, its main objective quickly became the overthrow of the Nicaraguan government.

Determined to defeat the Sandinistas, the Reagan administration evaded a Congressional prohibition on the use of US funds to overthrow the government of Nicaragua by maintaining that its purpose in supporting the Contras was to pressure the Sandinistas to negotiate with their opponents and to stop aiding the Salvadoran guerrillas. After the Contra force had grown to around 12,000 troops and had, with CIA help, engaged in some well-publicized attacks on Nicaraguan targets, the US Congress, in May 1984, prohibited all aid to them. (The prohibition was to go into effect on October 1, 1984.) Rather than stop supporting the Contras, the Reagan administration turned to foreign governments and private sources for funds, and, in a controversial and illegal action, diverted to the Contras profits derived from the secret sale of arms to Iran. Exposed in late 1986, this operation, which became known as the Iran–Contra Affair, led to the resignation and later conviction of several of Reagan's top aides. Although Reagan himself escaped indictment, the affair undermined support for his policies and might have made him more willing to reach arms control agreements with the Soviets.

Meanwhile, in the fall of 1983, efforts by Mexico, Colombia, Panama, and Venezuela (known as the Contadora Group, after the island where they first met) resulted in a Central American peace plan that promised to end the conflicts that plagued the region. The key elements of the plan were free elections in all participating countries, an end to outside military assistance, withdrawal of foreign military advisers, elimination of foreign military bases, and cessation of all aid to forces seeking to destabilize or overthrow regional governments. The Reagan administration opposed the plan because it accepted the Sandinista regime and put limits on US involvement in an area where the United States was accustomed to operating without external constraints. Although the region's governments, including the Nicaraguan government, endorsed the plan, the United States was able to prevent its implementation.

The Sandinistas had enjoyed fairly broad public support in the first few years following the revolution. Access to education and health care expanded, and the government moved slowly and cautiously in implementing economic reforms, initially limiting nationalization to properties owned by the Somoza family and its close supporters. Increased Contra activity, however, harmed the economy, which had not recovered from the devastation inflicted during the revolution, and forced the government to divert a larger and larger portion of the national budget to defense. And, as the Contra attacks increased, government toleration of dissent decreased. Nevertheless, the Sandinista candidate won over 60 percent of the vote in November 1984 elections. Although turnout was high (around 75 percent) and international observers certified the elections as free and fair, the FSLN victory was tainted by the withdrawal, at US insistence, of the main opposition candidate. To increase the pressure on the Sandinistas further, Reagan issued an executive order in May 1985 imposing an economic embargo on Nicaragua.

Although US pressure on Nicaragua exacted a heavy toll, the Sandinistas remained in power. The United States was more successful in Grenada where a US invasion overthrew a leftist government in October 1983. Four years earlier, in March 1979, a vaguely Marxist–Leninist group known as the New JEWEL Movement had seized control of the tiny Caribbean island. (JEWEL was an acronym for Joint Endeavor for Welfare, Education, and Liberation of the People.) The new government, led by Maurice Bishop, soon alienated the United States by adopting a radical foreign policy and turning to Cuba, the Soviet Union, and other communist states for assistance. The United States also alleged that an airport, which was being built on Grenada with Cuban, as well as Venezuelan and European Community, assistance, was intended for Soviet and Cuban military use. Bishop denied this, pointing out that a larger airport was needed to expand Grenada's tourist trade.

The removal and execution of the popular Bishop by rivals in the ruling group in mid-October 1983 provided the United States with an opportunity to remove a hostile government. Citing concerns for the safety of several hundred US citizens in Grenada (mostly students at a US-run medical school), and the support of Grenada's neighbors, President Reagan dispatched 1,900 US troops to Grenada on October 25. Encountering little resistance, US forces quickly gained control of the island, arrested what was left of the Grenadian government, and, after a brief occupation, organized elections, which were held the following year. Although popular in the United States, the US action was condemned by the United Nations, with only a US veto preventing a Security Council censure.

The invasion of Grenada, coupled with increases in support for the Contras and the Afghan resistance led to a codification of US policy toward the Third World which became known as the Reagan Doctrine. In an ironic reversal of the situation during most of the Cold War, the heart of the Reagan Doctrine was US support for anti-communist insurgents fighting against Soviet-supported governments. (Until the revolutionary wave of the 1970s, only a few communist governments were in power in the Third World.) Building on the Carter administration's human rights policy, the Reagan Doctrine stressed US support for democracy and human rights in the Third World and adamant opposition to terrorism. Although many, if not most, of the groups receiving US aid under the Reagan Doctrine were themselves anti-democratic and guilty of human rights abuses and terrorist activities, this focus proved successful because most of the target governments were, to varying degrees, also guilty of similar offenses. In addition, the Reagan administration aggressively promoted free market economics policies as an antidote to the statist development policies common in the Third World. The Third World debt crisis, which had emerged in the early 1980s, put many Third World governments at the mercy of their creditors and forced them to accept the free market prescriptions of the United States, the International Monetary Fund, and the World Bank.

The Reagan administration continued the Carter administration's support of the mujahedin's resistance to Soviet occupation, providing around $2 billion in military and economic assistance. Pakistan was key to the US effort, providing both a base for the rebels and a conduit for US aid. In addition, the PRC and Egypt played key roles, supplying Soviet-made or -designed weapons for the resistance, though the United States paid the Chinese for much of their "aid." The United States increased the amount of its aid in 1985, and in 1986 began supplying more sophisticated weaponry, including its most advanced hand-held anti-aircraft missile, the "Stinger." Although Stingers were effective against Soviet and Afghan government aircraft and helicopters, the mujahedin also used them to shoot down at least one civilian passenger plane, and some were diverted to other groups.

In July 1985, at the same time as it was increasing aid to the Afghan resistance, the Reagan administration secured the repeal of earlier Congressional legislation prohibiting CIA involvement in Angola. This allowed the United States to provide military and economic assistance to guerrilla forces led by UNITA (the National Union for the Total Independence of Angola), which, with South African assistance, had been fighting the Marxist-led government of Angola since 1975. Aid to UNITA was part of the Reagan administration's policy of "constructive engagement" with the white-minority government of South Africa. This policy was based on reaching an accommodation with the South African government in order to protect US economic and security interests in the region. The United States also sent aid to non-communist resistance groups in Cambodia, which, along with the Chinese-supported Khmer Rouge, were battling the government installed by the Vietnamese in 1978.

Support for anti-communist movements was not limited to the Third World. The United States also provided extensive covert financial and other assistance to the Solidarity independent trade union in Poland. In August 1980, after a wave of strikes and factory occupations, the communist government of Poland had agreed to legalize Solidarity. In addition to lacking legitimacy, a characteristic it shared with the other communist regimes in Eastern Europe, the Polish government faced widespread discontent due to failed economic policies that had saddled Poland with a massive debt to Western lenders. With political authority deteriorating and unrest spreading, the Soviets put pressure on Polish communist leaders to bring the situation under control or run the risk of Soviet military intervention. Given its size and location, a stable, friendly Poland was critical to the Soviet security position in Eastern Europe. With a Warsaw Pact intervention apparently imminent, Polish Prime Minister General Wojciech Jaruzelski, who was also defense minister and head of the ruling United Workers' Party, declared a state of siege on December 13, 1981, and ordered the arrest of more than 5,000 opposition leaders. Jaruzelski's actions probably prevented Soviet intervention and restored a degree of stability, at least in the short run.[4]

During 1981, the United States and its NATO allies had issued several warnings against Soviet military intervention in Poland. In response to the imposition of martial law the Western countries canceled plans to renegotiate Poland's debt and announced that they would not extend new credits. The United States imposed additional trade sanctions on Poland, and later suspended Poland's most favored nation trade status and blocked International Monetary Fund loans to Poland. Although the Soviets had refrained from direct intervention, the United States also imposed a number of economic sanctions on the Soviet Union, including suspension of sales of oil and gas technology and licenses for various high-technology exports.

The Reagan administration viewed the sanctions against the Soviet Union not only as punishment for Soviet pressures on Poland, but as a way to damage the Soviet economy and reduce its capacity to support Soviet military power and meet the needs of its citizens. In June 1982, the Reagan administration expanded the sanctions to cover US equipment and technology for construction of a Soviet gas pipeline to Western Europe, including equipment manufactured by European firms under US licenses. The major Western European nations protested the US action as an illegal attempt to impose extraterritorial trade sanctions and rejected the US argument that the proposed pipeline could provide the Soviets with a means of applying economic pressure on Western Europe by threatening to withhold supplies. Some Europeans suspected that the United States opposed the pipeline because it reduced US leverage over Western Europe by providing an East–West economic link that supported European détente. European opposition forced the United States to withdraw the extended trade sanctions in return for promises of vigilance in trade matters.[5]

After some initial hesitation, the United States and the PRC renewed strategic cooperation against the Soviet Union. President Reagan and many of his advisers had long-standing attachments to the Nationalist regime in Taiwan and regarded the Chinese Communists with great suspicion. In addition, compared to Taiwan, from which the United States could project its power throughout East Asia and the Western Pacific, the PRC seemed to offer few advantages. Although the PRC had a large army, technological backwardness reduced the value of its air force and missile arsenal, and its navy was small and weak. PRC leaders also had doubts about the value of a strategic partnership with the United States. The collapse of détente had removed the danger of Soviet–American cooperation against the PRC and allowed the Chinese to adopt a more independent foreign policy. The PRC criticized US policy in Central America, offered no support to the Solidarity movement in Poland, and supported the Soviet position against SDI.

On the other hand, PRC leaders had begun to implement a number of market reforms in the late 1970s, and desired access to US trade, technology, and credits. Likewise, the United States needed PRC help in supporting the Afghan insurgents and for putting pressure on the Vietnamese in Cambodia. After resolving a disagreement over the US right to sell arms to Taiwan, the United States in May 1983 granted the PRC greater access to US civilian technology, opening the way for President Reagan's visit to China in April 1984. Although Reagan stressed that the two nations had a common interest in opposing Soviet expansion, the Sino-American strategic relationship did not return to the high point of 1978–80. Economic ties increased, however, and by the mid-1980s, Sino-American trade had become far more important than the trade of either with the Soviet Union.

GORBACHEV AND THE END OF THE COLD WAR

US initiatives dominated the first half of the 1980s. Soviet policy, in part because of problems caused by the deaths in quick succession of three leaders – Brezhnev in November 1982, Yuri Andropov in February 1984, and Konstantin Chernenko in March 1985 – was largely reactive. The final years of the Cold War, in contrast, were dominated by Soviet leader Mikhail Gorbachev, who came to power in March 1985.

Gorbachev inherited a situation characterized by declining economic performance, a widening technology gap with the West, an increasingly demoralized population, and a confrontational and counterproductive foreign policy. Although the heart of his policies was open debate on government policies (glasnost) and economic restructuring (perestroika), his internal and foreign policies were deeply interrelated. Gorbachev and his colleagues believed that without some kind of democratic renewal and economic transformation the Soviet Union would not be able to remain internationally competitive. In addition, ending the Cold War and forging a new and less competitive relationship with the West was crucial to the success of perestroika. A less confrontational foreign policy would permit far lower defense spending and allow the Soviet Union to devote greater attention and resources to internal economic reform. In addition, Stalin and his successors had used the Cold War to justify internal repression, and continuation of the Cold War could block needed reforms. Moreover, Gorbachev and his colleagues believed that continued coercive control of Eastern Europe, a security imperative of a confrontational security policy, was incompatible with democratization and economic reform in the Soviet Union.[6]

Gorbachev focused first on arms control. Soviet leaders and defense planners, recognizing that military expenditures were crippling the Soviet economy without providing increased security, came to the conclusion that a limited number of nuclear weapons provided sufficient security against both a US nuclear attack and against any possible invasion by conventional forces. Arms control would reduce military expenditures and, equally importantly, reduce tensions with the West and allow an overall improvement in relations.

The United States and the Soviet Union had resumed arms control talks in early 1985, after Reagan and his new secretary of state George Shultz abandoned their earlier emphasis on winning the arms race and decided to test the Soviets' willingness to curtail competition in nuclear weapons. Gorbachev moved quickly to take the initiative. In April, he suspended the countermeasures applied in response to the NATO INF deployments and halted further deployment of SS-20s. In August, he announced a unilateral moratorium on nuclear testing, and offered to extend it indefinitely if the United States would also stop testing. Gorbachev and Reagan met in Geneva in November 1985. Although the two leaders succeeded in establishing a personal relationship, they failed to reach any agreements. In January 1986, Gorbachev unveiled a plan for complete nuclear disarmament to take place in three stages by the year 2000. Stage One proposed that the United States and the Soviet Union reduce their intermediate-range (theater) nuclear forces to zero, and did not mention British, French, and Chinese forces. At the Reykjavik summit in October 1986, Gorbachev offered to remove all SS-20s from Europe and limit the number deployed in Asia to 100. He also proposed a plan to cut US and Soviet strategic nuclear forces in half. Although the two leaders almost reached agreement on eliminating nuclear weapons entirely, Reagan's dogged defense of SDI, which the Soviets continued to view as incompatible with mutual security, prevented any agreement.

Following Reykjavik, Gorbachev dropped his previous insistence that agreement on SDI was a prerequisite for progress on all arms control matters and accepted the "zero option" proposal made by the United States in 1981. In April 1987, Gorbachev suggested that, in addition to eliminating all intermediate-range forces held by both sides, they eliminate a category of shorter-range intermediate forces (those with a range of 500–1,000 kilometers as opposed to the first category's range of 1,000–5,000 kilometers). This proposal, dubbed the "double zero" option, became the basis for the Intermediate Nuclear Forces (INF) Treaty signed in Washington in December 1987.

The INF Treaty marked the first arms reduction (as opposed to arms limitation) agreement of the Cold War. Building on this momentum, Gorbachev turned his attention to conventional forces. After NATO rejected his July 1988 call for a "pan-European Reykjavik" (deep cuts in both sides' force levels), Gorbachev, in a December address before the United Nations, announced a 12 percent unilateral reduction in total Soviet conventional forces, including a 20 percent reduction in forces west of the Urals. Moreover, around 50,000 troops and some 5,000 tanks would come from Soviet forces in Eastern Europe, significantly reducing the Warsaw Pact's offensive capabilities.

The cutbacks, which were to be completed by 1991, grew out of a drastic revision of Soviet military strategy that replaced the previous objective of not losing a war with the West with the objective of preventing such a war. The old strategy required a conventional capacity configured for offensive action and had proved counterproductive, as NATO had built up its conventional and nuclear forces in response. The Soviets hoped that switching to a defensive posture would provide more security by improving relations with the West as well as allowing reductions in military spending. The new strategy also had important implications for Soviet policy toward Eastern Europe.

Control of Eastern Europe was vital to Soviet security under the old strategy of not losing a world war. Without a large number of offensively structured forces in Eastern Europe, and especially in East Germany, it would be very difficult for the Soviets to win a conventional war in Europe, as required under the old strategy. Soviet forces in Eastern Europe also served to maintain pro-Soviet governments in power. Lacking legitimacy, the region's communist regimes rested on a "foundation of coercion." And, as economic conditions worsened and the gap between Eastern and Western Europe widened, opposition to communist rule increased.

The new Soviet security strategy no longer required maintaining a sphere of influence in Eastern Europe. Moreover, as Gorbachev and his reformist colleagues struggled to restructure the Soviet economy and open up its political system, they became more and more aware that trying to maintain coercive control of Eastern Europe could undermine their efforts at internal reform. Economic factors also played an important role. The cost of economic subsidies to Eastern Europe had long been a huge drain on Soviet resources. One of the most important and costly subsidies was Soviet sale of oil and natural gas to Eastern Europe at prices below world market levels. Oil and gas exports were a key source of hard currency for the Soviet Union, especially after world prices skyrocketed in the 1970s due to turmoil in the Middle East. As prices dropped sharply in the early 1980s, however, the Soviet Union cut back energy deliveries to Eastern Europe in order to maintain the level of its export earnings. This decision exacerbated the problems faced by Eastern Europe's economies, most of which owed large debts to Western creditors.

The end of Soviet control of Eastern Europe occurred first in Poland. The largest and most anti-Soviet country in Eastern Europe, Poland had been the scene of popular mobilizations that forced changes in government in 1956, 1970, and 1981. Following the imposition of martial law in December 1981, widespread public support, the encouragement of the Catholic Church, covert assistance from the West, and continuing economic difficulties led to the re-emergence of the organized opposition as a potent political force. The defeat of a government-sponsored referendum on economic reform in 1987 and widespread strikes in 1988 underlined the need for national reconciliation to deal with Poland's problems, and forced the Jaruzelski government to open up the political system. June 1989 national elections, conducted under a semi-democratic formula that guaranteed a communist majority in the lower house of parliament, resulted in an overwhelming victory for the opposition and the appointment of a non-communist prime minister in August. While the presidency, the interior and defense ministries, and the lower house of parliament remained under communist control, Poland and Eastern Europe had a non-communist government for the first time in over forty years.

Already a regional leader in implementing economic reforms, Hungary legalized opposition political parties in January 1989. Then, in September, the Hungarian government reached an agreement with the opposition to hold free elections in six months. The following month, the Hungarian communists, who a year earlier had replaced long-time leader János Kádár, split, and the reformers formed a new party dedicated to democracy, legality, and socialism.

As part of the democratic opening in Hungary, the Hungarian government had opened its borders with the West. This decision allowed East Germans to take advantage of Hungary's border with Austria to flee to the West without risk. Growing numbers of refugees and massive demonstrations in Berlin, Leipzig, and other cities put enormous pressure on the East German government. After Gorbachev warned the East German communist leadership that he would not support repression, the party ousted its aging hardline leader and appointed a new government under reformist leadership. The new government, faced with continuing demonstrations, ended all restrictions on travel to the West. On the night of November 9–10, 1989, thousands of East Germans poured into West Berlin, as the Berlin Wall, pre-eminent symbol of the Cold War division of Germany and Europe, was breached. The following month, the East German government ended the communist monopoly of power and announced free elections to be held in March 1990.

The same day that the Berlin Wall came down, the Bulgarian Communist Party deposed its longtime leader and promised reforms and free elections. Although the Bulgarian Communists managed to stay in power until the following year, events moved much faster in Czechoslovakia. Emboldened by events in neighboring states, massive demonstrations and a general strike led to the appointment of a non-communist government on December 10. Three weeks later opposition leader Vaclav Havel became president.

Only in Romania did the collapse of communist rule result in significant bloodshed. After Romanian dictator Nicolae Ceauşescu's security forces opened fire on demonstrators in the city of Timisoara, massive demonstrations erupted in other areas, including the capital, Bucharest. On December 21, with military units beginning to support the demonstrations, Ceauşescu and his wife attempted unsuccessfully to flee the country. After a hurried trial, they were executed on December 25, and a National Salvation Front, led by a former interior minister, took power.

By the end of 1989, every pro-Soviet communist regime in Eastern Europe had collapsed. Although the "revolutions of 1989" had resulted in far more rapid and drastic changes than the Soviet leadership had expected, they came about peacefully (with the exception of Romania) and without direct confrontation with the more than 500,000 Soviet troops stationed throughout the region. The Soviets had rejected the alternative of repression as doomed in the long run and as incompatible with liberalization in the Soviet Union. Indeed, at crucial junctures in Poland and East Germany, Gorbachev not only opposed the use of force, but actively promoted political liberalization even when it resulted in the collapse of communist control.

The following year, the Soviets, albeit reluctantly, accepted German reunification as well as its membership in NATO. The treaty providing for reunification contained several safeguards insisted on by the Soviets, including a limit on the size of Germany's armed forces and a prohibition of German possession of atomic, biological, or chemical weapons. NATO also pledged to reduce its forces and to make its nuclear forces weapons of last resort. The Soviets agreed to withdraw their forces from Germany, with Germany providing economic assistance for the withdrawal. The treaty was signed on September 12, 1990, and on October 3, the Federal Republic absorbed East Germany.

The following month, after lengthy negotiations, NATO and the Warsaw Pact signed a treaty drastically reducing the size and armament of their conventional forces in Europe. The Warsaw Pact, and the Soviet Union in particular, accepted deeper cuts in their forces than those required of NATO and the United States. By the time the United States ratified the treaty in November 1991, the Warsaw Pact had ceased to exist, its members having voted earlier in the year to cancel all military agreements. The Warsaw Pact was formally dissolved on July 1, three days after its economic counterpart, the Council on Mutual Economic Assistance, was liquidated by the common consent of its members.

At the same time as Gorbachev was taking the momentous actions that resulted in the end of the Cold War in Europe, he was working to repair relations with the PRC. China was moving toward a more independent foreign policy posture and had identified three obstacles to improved relations: the Soviet military build-up in Asia; Soviet troops in Afghanistan; and Vietnamese troops in Cambodia. As noted earlier, the 1987 INF Treaty eliminated Soviet intermediate-range missiles from Asia as well as from Europe. And, as part of his overall reduction in the level of Soviet conventional forces, Gorbachev reduced the number of Soviet troops on China's borders, and removed Soviet troops from Mongolia.

Almost from the outset, the Soviet dilemma in Afghanistan had been to find a way to disengage honorably while ensuring a friendly, non-aligned Afghanistan. In February 1988, Gorbachev announced his intention to pull all Soviet troops out the country. Negotiations under UN auspices resulted in a series of agreements in the spring of 1988 that committed the Soviet Union to withdraw its forces by February 15, 1989. Although the Reagan administration had earlier agreed to stop aiding the Afghan insurgents when Soviet troops left, it announced in March 1988 that the United States would continue to provide aid to the mujahedin while the Soviets provided aid to the Afghan government. Thus, although Soviet forces left on schedule in February 1989, the war continued for three more years. After the United States and the Soviet Union agreed to cut off all arms shipments at the end of 1991, the Afghan government fell in April 1992. Fighting continued among the various factions of the resistance, however.

In addition to removing Soviet forces from Afghanistan, Gorbachev successfully pressured the Vietnamese to withdraw their troops from Cambodia. Around half of the 100,000 Vietnamese in Cambodia were gone by the end of 1988, with the remainder leaving in September 1989. The Soviets also began to phase out their military assistance to Vietnam and to withdraw their forces from bases at Cam Ranh Bay and Danang. The various Cambodian factions reached a peace agreement under UN auspices in October 1990.

The pattern of regional settlements continued in Africa, where Soviet and American negotiators helped mediate a settlement linking the withdrawal of all foreign forces from Angola with Namibian independence. The December 1988 agreements provided for the withdrawal of all foreign forces from Angola by mid-1991, and South African acceptance of a UN-sponsored plan for Namibian independence, which occurred in March 1990. South African forces had already withdrawn from Angola by the time the accords were signed, and all Cuban troops left by June 1991. As in Afghanistan, fighting continued in Angola as the United States continued to aid the UNITA rebels and the Soviet Union continued to send arms to the Angolan government. A May 1991 peace accord, brokered by the United States, the Soviet Union, and Portugal, temporarily ended the fighting and provided for elections and national reconciliation. After the MPLA won the October 1992 national elections, however, UNITA resumed the civil war.

The Soviets began cutting back military assistance and withdrawing their advisers from Ethiopia in 1990. The Cubans withdrew their combat forces and advisers at the same time. After the Ethiopian government fell to regional rebels in May 1991, the Soviets evacuated their base in the Dahlak Islands.

Although aided by the changes in Soviet policies, the cease-fire and settlement in Central America were primarily the result of a regional peace effort led by Costa Rican President Oscar Arias Sánchez. Building on the earlier efforts by the Contadora Group, Arias proposed a plan that called for cease-fires in each of the war-torn nations in the region, free elections, and the ending of all aid to irregular forces or insurrectionary movements. Accepted by the region's governments in 1987, the Arias peace plan became the basis for ending the Cold War in Central America.

Under pressure from the United States, which continued to support the Contras and refused to relax economic sanctions, and faced with a cut-off of Soviet aid, the Sandinistas agreed to hold free elections in February 1990. After nine years of warfare that cost over 31,000 lives, the Nicaraguan economy was in ruins, the effects of the fighting and economic sanctions compounded by runaway inflation. In addition, the Sandinista regime had lost much of its initial popularity due to restraints on civil and political liberties, corruption, and the imposition of a military draft. The United States both openly and covertly financed the opposition campaign, and warned that a Sandinista victory would result in the continuation of US economic sanctions and possibly resumption of the Contra war, which had largely wound down after 1987. Finally, the opposition candidate, Violeta Barrios de Chamorro, the widow of a victim of Somoza's dictatorship and a member of the first post-Somoza government, stressed national reconciliation rather than reversal of the revolution. Chamorro and her coalition won a clear majority in the internationally supervised elections. While the Sandinistas remained the single largest and best-organized party and retained control of the army, they accepted the results and turned over power to the victorious opposition.

The momentous changes set in motion by Gorbachev thus ended the Cold War well before the Soviet Union disintegrated in December 1991. The collapse of the Soviet Union, while closely bound up with the Cold War, was also the long-delayed result of a process of disintegration of multinational empires that was one of the key legacies of World War I. While that war destroyed other empires, the Tsarist empire had continued under "new management" as the Soviet Union. Although the Soviet Union was not initially affected by the end of European empires set in motion by World War II, eventually both processes caught up with the last of the great multinational and colonial empires. In the end, nationalism and democratization proved incompatible with empire, dooming the Soviet Union.

While most scholars agree that the Cold War ended when the leaders of the Soviet Union decided it was no longer worth fighting, the reasons for the shift in Soviet policies are still in dispute. Reagan supporters and some scholars claim that the Soviets shifted to less confrontational policies in response to the US military build-up and political offensive. In this view, US actions raised the costs of confrontation and forced the Soviets into a corner from which there was no escape save for surrender.[7] Other scholars argue that the new generation of Soviet leaders that emerged in the 1980s had already concluded that the policies of their predecessors had been counterproductive and that continued conflict threatened their goal of overcoming the disastrous legacy of Stalinism, reforming their economy, democratizing their politics, and revitalizing their society. According to this analysis, US actions did not cause the changes in Soviet domestic and foreign policies and might have delayed them by providing opponents of reform with arguments against better relations with the West and relaxation of internal controls.[8] Although this debate is not likely to be resolved for some time, it raises questions that are relevant to understanding the history of the Cold War.

7   Understanding the Cold War

This study has analyzed the Cold War as a product of the domestic histories of the great powers and of the structure and dynamics of international relations. Following World War II, changes in the global distribution of power, weapons technology, the balance of political forces within and among nations, the world economy, and relations between the industrialized nations and the underdeveloped periphery led to the Cold War. Further changes in these areas perpetuated it, and eventually brought about its end.

Throughout the Cold War, the global distribution of power influenced US and Soviet perceptions of their respective national interests and consequently their actions. Despite the upsurge in Soviet military power in the 1970s and a relative decline in US economic strength, the global distribution of power remained tilted against the Soviet Union throughout the Cold War. If popular support, industrial infrastructure, skilled manpower, and technological prowess are factored into the definition of power, the postwar era was bipolar only in a narrow military sense. By any broad definition of power, the Soviet Union remained throughout the Cold War an "incomplete superpower."[1]

This imbalance emerges even more starkly when the strength of the Western alliance is measured against that of the Soviet Bloc. Even in military terms the Soviet position had as many elements of weakness as of strength. Throughout the Cold War, the Soviet Union and its Warsaw Pact allies possessed numerical superiority in ground forces along the central front in the heart of Europe. In addition, Soviet and Chinese Communist ground forces outnumbered any possible opponent in Northeast Asia during the 1950s. In the 1970s, the Soviet Union also achieved rough parity with the United States in strategic nuclear weapons.[2] On the other hand, the Soviet Union was never able to count on the loyalty of its Warsaw Pact partners, and after the Sino-Soviet split in the late 1950s almost a third of its ground forces had to be deployed along its border with the PRC. In assessing the nuclear balance, the Soviets had to take into account the arsenals of the other nuclear powers – Great Britain, France, and the PRC – as well as that of the United States.

The Soviet strategic position worsened over time relatively as well as absolutely. Although the weakening of German and Japanese power initially improved the Soviet Union's relative position, the defeat of these two powers along with the decline of Britain and France left undisputed leadership of the non-communist world to the United States. The successful reconstruction of West Germany and Japan, the economic recovery of the countries of Western Europe, and their incorporation into a US-led alliance meant that four of the world's five centers of industrial might stayed outside Soviet control. Moreover, the PRC's break with the USSR in the late 1950s and the growing hostility between the two communist giants put enormous demands on the Soviet military, strains that the Soviet economy eventually could not bear. The Sino-Soviet split ended any possibility of communism constituting an alternative world system that could compete with the capitalist West.

Closely related to the global distribution of power, the arms race was one of the most dynamic aspects of the Cold War. World War II accelerated dramatic changes in the technology of warfare. The systematic application of science to warfare produced weapons that reached new heights of destructiveness and dramatically expanded power projection capabilities. The development of atomic and hydrogen bombs and ballistic missiles magnified the destructive capacity of warfare and exposed most of the globe to attack and devastation. At various times, technological advances threatened to give one superpower or the other a dangerous edge over its rival, thereby triggering vigorous countermeasures and increasing the risk of nuclear disaster. The resulting arms race led to ever higher levels of military spending, more destabilizing technological competition, and constantly growing nuclear arsenals. Moreover, military expenditures tended to create constituencies that benefitted from the continuation of Cold War tensions. Established early in the Cold War, this pattern of action and counteraction continued to its end.

Although some analysts have argued that atomic weapons and the near certainty of retaliation may have helped prevent a war between the superpowers, they did not prevent numerous non-nuclear conflicts in the Third World. In addition, there were deep flaws in the command and control systems of both superpowers. As one scholar has noted, "not only were safety procedures inherently subject to error but the necessity to maintain active readiness and the capacity to respond to a nuclear attack inevitably pushed safety to the limit."[3] With both US and Soviet nuclear forces geared to "launch on warning," the danger of an accidental nuclear war was extremely high.

Gradually, the leaders of the United States and the Soviet Union came to terms with the implications of the nuclear revolution. Nuclear wars, they eventually realized, might be fought, but they could not be won. While possession of nuclear weapons might help expand influence abroad and deter encroachments on their truly vital interests, marginal increments in nuclear weaponry did not provide commensurate additional leverage in the struggle for international influence. More and better weapons often decreased rather than increased security.

The history of the arms race highlights the impact of what international relations scholars call the security dilemma. Actions taken by one nation for its security can easily be construed by its adversary as threatening and lead to countermeasures that further reduce security for both sides. The workings of the security dilemma had an especially stark impact on the Soviet Union. Most of the measures the Soviets adopted to enhance their security resulted in less security because they provoked countermeasures by the more powerful United States and its allies that preserved or increased Western supremacy.[4]

The potential for conflict inherent in the security dilemma was exacerbated by the different social, economic, and political systems of the two main protagonists. The Cold War was an economic as well as a military and political conflict, and geopolitical alignment almost always involved a choice of economic system. The interconnected nature of international issues and domestic dynamics was one of the most distinctive features of the Cold War. During the Cold War, the direction of social and economic development was the subject of great contention. The potential impact of internal political alignments on the global balance of power invested domestic political struggles with international political and strategic significance. Changes in the balance of political forces both within and among nations took place throughout the Cold War and played a major role in initiating, prolonging, and finally ending the conflict.

The collapse of communism as an ideology paralleled the decline in the Soviet strategic position. Highly regarded by many at the end of World War II, the appeal of communism and the Soviet model of development declined sharply in most of the world over the course of the Cold War. Repression in the Soviet Union, Eastern Europe, and the People's Republic of China tarnished communism's image. In the 1960s and 1970s some European communist parties attempted to reform themselves and to divorce communism from the harsh reality of Soviet (and

Chinese) practice. These efforts failed to gain sufficient support to wrest leadership of world communism from the Soviet Union and the PRC. The faltering Soviet economy further discredited communism's appeal, as did growing international awareness of human rights and environmental abuses inside the Soviet Union, Eastern Europe, and the PRC.

Transnational ideological conflict was closely related to the development of national economies and the evolution of the global economy. Economic changes restructured power relationships among as well as within nations. The inability of the Soviet Union's economy to compete with the West restricted its citizens' standard of living, threatened its national security, and ultimately eroded the legitimacy of the communist system. Although the roots of Soviet economic problems go back at least to the emergence of the Stalinist system in the late 1920s, military competition with the United States and the PRC forced the Soviets to devote a much larger share of their smaller gross national product to defense, and siphoned off resources needed for economic modernization and development. The diversion of investment away from productive sectors and consumer goods ultimately undermined the Soviet Union's willingness and ability to compete with the United States and to maintain its empire. Economic growth in the Soviet Bloc, which had risen in the late 1940s and the 1950s, began to slow in the early 1970s and never recovered.

The failure of communism to deliver the goods contrasted sharply with Western consumer culture. Many among the new generation of Soviet citizens measured their economic status against that of their counterparts in the West rather than that of their parents, most of whom had witnessed significant improvements in living standards in their lifetimes. The 1986 Chernobyl nuclear disaster and subsequent cover-up attempts delivered a major blow to communist rule by demoralizing the few who still believed the system could be transformed from within. By the end of the 1980s, the Soviet system inspired and attracted almost no one, especially those who knew it best.

The reconstruction, reform, and relative resilience of the world capitalist system contrasted sharply with the failure of communism. On the defensive in 1945 due to the depth and duration of the Great Depression and its association with fascism, capitalism underwent significant changes and staged a remarkable comeback. The United States supported the reconstruction of Western Europe and Japan, promoted economic integration, helped forge a stable global financial order, and encouraged international trade and investment through the lowering of tariffs and the removal of other impediments to the free flow of goods and capital. Although the Western economies continued to suffer periods of stagnation and glaring inequalities in the distribution of income and wealth, they experienced unprecedented economic growth in the 1950s and 1960s and functioned sufficiently well thereafter to sustain their military might, support increasingly inclusive welfare states, and legitimize Western political and economic institutions.

While the oil crises of the 1970s caused economic difficulties and financial disorder in the West, the Soviets did not gain any lasting advantages from them. As an oil exporter, the Soviet Union benefitted briefly from higher oil prices, but the windfall distracted attention from the need for structural reforms. In the mid-1980s, when the Soviet Union finally had a government interested in economic reforms, international oil prices collapsed. The vitality of the West German and Japanese economies and the emergence of such Western-oriented "newly industrializing countries" as Taiwan and South Korea ensured the West's economic dominance over the Soviet Union and its allies, even as U.S technological and financial leadership declined and the US share of world production decreased.

The prosperity associated with the long boom stretching from the late 1940s to the early 1970s alleviated the excesses of prewar capitalism, undercut the appeal of leftist and communist parties, supported the ascendancy of moderate elites who associated their own well-being with that of the United States, and sustained the cohesion of the Western alliance. The defeat of the far right in World War II helped reduce divisions among non-communist elements, facilitating, at least in Western Europe and Japan, the emergence of a consensus supporting some form of capitalist welfare state and alignment with the United States. In addition, the Cold War provided a justification for the repression and marginalization of indigenous communist and other radical groups in the name of national security.

The Cold War distorted the process by which colonies gained their independence, and made decolonization more difficult and more violent. In addition, the Cold War polarized efforts at social, economic, and political change in Latin America. Although most conflicts in the Third World were largely indigenous in origin and their eventual success or failure was as much due to their internal histories and characteristics as to US and Soviet policies toward them, instability and conflict in the Third World fed Soviet–American rivalry.

The desire of many Third World independence movements to liberate their countries from foreign rule, to free their economies from foreign control, to overthrow repressive internal power structures put or kept in place by outside forces, and to challenge the West's cultural hegemony at times aligned some movements against the United States and its allies and with the Soviet Union. Western leaders feared that Third World radicalism could lead to the loss of access to raw materials, oil, food sources, and markets needed to rebuild the economies of Western Europe and Japan and to ensure continued US prosperity. Western leaders also feared that the Soviet Union would be able to gain ground through alliances with national liberation movements or in the turmoil that would accompany the end of Western control.

The Soviets proved unable to turn conditions in the Third World to their advantage, however. The era of decolonization (1945–75) represented a window of opportunity for the Soviet Union and a window of vulnerability for the United States and its allies. Although communist parties eventually came to power in some Third World countries (often among the poorest ones), these gains were either marginal or ephemeral as most national liberation movements proved to be beyond the control of any outside power. Soviet involvement in the Third World also galvanized Western counteractions. By the 1980s the declining competitiveness of the Soviet economy and unpromising experience with Soviet-style planning in the Third World and elsewhere left Third World countries with little choice but to abide by the economic rules set by the Western-dominated International Monetary Fund and World Bank and to look to the United States and its allies for capital, technology, and markets. By the end of the Cold War, the threat that Third World radicalism would weaken the West and add to Soviet power had dissipated.

Although the Soviet–American rivalry that was at the core of the Cold War ended with the collapse of Soviet power and the disintegration of the Soviet Union and its empire, controversies over the meaning of the Cold War have continued. Some writers celebrate US victory in the Cold War and argue that its outcome vindicates US policies and actions during the Cold War. Others emphasize the high costs of waging the Cold War, and argue that less confrontational US policies would have brought about the same or a better outcome earlier and at a lower cost. These are very difficult issues to resolve. For one thing, the availability of Soviet documents is still very limited and incomplete. Moreover, the meaning of many of the few documents that are available is ambiguous. In many cases, as one scholar has noted, the same Soviet behavior can be interpreted as either expansionist or defensive.[5] Although many more US documents are available, especially for the 1940s and 1950s, full documentation on some key aspects of US policy, especially covert action, is still not available. In addition, the meaning of many US actions is also ambiguous. The doctrine of containment, the overarching principle of US Cold War foreign policy not only aimed at limiting the expansion of Soviet power and influence but also facilitated the expansion of US power and influence.[6] This brief book cannot resolve these controversies, which are rooted in deep, though often unacknowledged, ideological and philosophical differences. Hopefully, however, it provides sufficient information for readers to reach their own conclusions on these and other important issues.

Any assessment of the wisdom of the Cold War must take its costs into account.[7] The United States, the Soviet Union, and many other countries suffered great harm from waging it. With its insatiable demand on resources, its exacerbation of ideological and political intolerance, its emphasis on external threats, and its consequent neglect of internal problems, the Cold War deformed US, Soviet, and other societies, distorted their priorities, and dissipated their wealth. The Cold War also exacerbated such problems as chronic poverty, environmental degradation, ethnic conflict, and the proliferation of weapons of mass destruction. To paraphrase the seventeenth-century philosopher Thomas Hobbes, the Cold War was nasty, brutish, and long.[8]

Notes

2 THE COLD WAR BEGINS, 1945–50

1 NSC-68 can be found in United States Department of State, *Foreign Relations of the United States, 1950*, vol. 1 (Washington, DC: US Government Printing Office, 1977), 234–85.
2 See Stephen Walt, *The Origin of Alliances* (Ithaca, NY: Cornell University Press, 1987).
3 The sterling area was made up of the United Kingdom, its colonies and dominions (except Canada), and other countries (mostly in the Middle East) that conducted their international trade in sterling. As late as 1946, around half of the world's international transactions were conducted in sterling. See Sidney Pollard, *The International Economy since 1945* (London: Routledge, 1997), 95–96.
4 The impact of the depression was not limited to the developed countries. See Dietmar Rothermund, *The Global Impact of the Great Depression, 1929–39* (London: Routledge, 1996).
5 Following major clashes, the Soviet Union and Japan had signed a neutrality pact in April 1941.
6 See J. Samuel Walker, *Prompt and Utter Destruction: Truman and the Use of Atomic Bombs against Japan* (Chapel Hill, NC: University of North Carolina Press, 1997).
7 For the most complete discussion of the Soviet development of atomic weapons, including the controversial issue of espionage, see David Holloway, *Stalin and the Bomb: The Soviet Union and Atomic Energy, 1939–1956* (New Haven, CT: Yale University Press, 1994).
8 See Diane Shaver Clemens, *Yalta* (New York: Oxford University Press, 1970).
9 The classic statement of US security concerns is Melvyn P. Leffler, "The American Conception of National Security and the Origins of the Cold War, 1945–48," *American Historical Review* 89 (April 1984): 346–81; reprinted in Melvyn P. Leffler and David S. Painter, eds, *Origins of the Cold War: An International History* (London: Routledge, 1994).
10 The best place to follow the recent revelations about Soviet foreign policy is through the publications of the Cold War International History Project sponsored by the Woodrow Wilson Center in Washington, DC. In addition to their *Bulletin*, see also their website: www.cwihp.si.edu. See also the

symposium in *Diplomatic History* 21 (Spring 1997); and Melvyn P. Leffler, "Inside Enemy Archives: The Cold War Reopened," *Foreign Affairs* 75 (July/August 1996): 120–35. For an eloquent restatement of traditional views, see John Lewis Gaddis, *We Now Know: Rethinking Cold War History* (New York: Oxford University Press, 1997).

11 After 1947, a theoretical option would have been to relinquish control of Eastern Europe, join the Marshall Plan, and accept US influence over future Soviet economic development.

12 Under the European Recovery Program, the United States provided over $13 billion in aid to Western Europe between 1948 and 1952. The Western zones of Germany received additional aid through the US occupation authorities.

13 As James E. Cronin points out, Marshall Plan aid also helped reorient the geographical focus of Germany's foreign economic relations from Eastern Europe to Western Europe and the world economy; Cronin, *The World the Cold War Made: Order, Chaos, and the Return of History* (London: Routledge, 1996), 91.

14 See Cary Fraser, "Understanding American Policy toward the Decolonization of European Empires, 1945–64," *Diplomacy and Statecraft* 3 (March 1992): 105–25; and Wm. Roger Louis and Ronald Robinson, "The Imperialism of Decolonization," *Journal of Imperial and Commonwealth History* 22 (September 1994): 462–511.

15 See Benjamin O. Fordham, *Building the Cold War Consensus: The Political Economy of US National Security Policy, 1949–51* (Ann Arbor, MI: University of Michigan Press, 1998).

16 See the discussion in Melvyn P. Leffler, *The Specter of Communism: The United States and the Origins of the Cold War, 1917–1953* (New York: Hill & Wang, 1994), 97–98; and the *Cold War International History Project Bulletin* 6–7 (Winter 1996/97), which is devoted to the 'Cold War in Asia.'

3 COMPETITION AND COEXISTENCE, 1950–62

1 See James E. Cronin, *The World the Cold War Made: Order, Chaos, and the Return of History* (London: Routledge, 1996).

2 Albania broke relations with the Soviet Union in late 1961, but did not formally withdraw from the Warsaw Pact until 1968.

3 See the discussion in Martin Walker, *The Cold War: A History* (New York: Henry Holt and Company, 1994), 78–81.

4 See Frederic C. Deyo, ed., *The Political Economy of the New Asian Industrialism* (Ithaca, NY: Cornell University Press, 1987).

5 Although the B-36, deployed in mid-1948, was an intercontinental bomber, it was very slow and vulnerable to Soviet interceptors.

6 David Holloway, *Stalin and the Bomb: The Soviet Union and Atomic Energy, 1938–1956* (New Haven, CT: Yale University Press, 1994), 306–08.

7 Stephen I. Schwartz, ed., *Atomic Audit: The Cost and Consequences of U.S. Nuclear Weapons since 1940* (Washington, DC: Brookings Institution, 1998), 281.

8 The U2s operated from bases in Britain, Turkey, Japan, and Pakistan. The United States later sponsored U-2 flights originating in Taiwan to photograph the PRC.

9 Walker, *Cold War*, 168–69.

10 Around 70,000 French soldiers lost their lives in Indochina between 1946 and 1954. The war was so unpopular that the French Army did not send conscripts to fight there, relying instead on career soldiers, the Foreign Legion, and colonial troops.

11 See Piero Gleijeses, *Shattered Hope: The Guatemalan Revolution and the United States, 1944–1954* (Princeton, NJ: Princeton University Press, 1991).

4 FROM COLD WAR TO DÉTENTE, 1963–73

1 See the account in Michael MccGwire, *Military Objectives in Soviet Foreign Policy* (Washington, DC: Brookings Institution, 1987).

2 Some scholars believe that the Soviets may have contemplated a pre-emptive strike on Chinese nuclear facilities to remedy the situation.

3 Peter H. Smith, *Talons of the Eagle: Dynamics of US–Latin American Relations* (New York: Oxford University Press, 1996), 154.

4 Walter LaFeber notes that Johnson's statement updated a 1950 assertion by Edward Miller, the assistant secretary of state for inter-American affairs, that collective intervention under the Rio Pact or the Organization of American States Charter to prevent a communist takeover of any American state was justified. See LaFeber, *Inevitable Revolutions: The United States in Central America*, second edn (New York: W.W. Norton & Company, 1993), 95–97.

5 FROM DÉTENTE TO CONFRONTATION, 1973–80

1 See the discussion in Richard Ned Lebow and Janice Gross Stein, *We All Lost the Cold War* (Princeton, NJ: Princeton University Press, 1994).

2 The boycott was run by the Organization of Arab Petroleum Exporting Countries (OAPEC), not by OPEC.

3 See Piero Gleijeses, "Havana's Policy in Africa, 1959–1976: New Evidence from Cuban Archives," *Cold War International History Project Bulletin* 8–9 (Winter 1996/1997): 5–18.

4 See the discussion in Olav Njølstad, "Key of Keys? SALT II and the Breakdown of Détente," in Odd Arne Westad, ed., *The Fall of Détente: Soviet–American Relations during the Carter Years* (Oslo: Scandinavian University Press, 1997), 34–71.

5 See William Burr, ed., *The Kissinger Transcripts: Top Secret Talks with Beijing and Moscow* (New York: New Press, 1999).

6 See Ronald E. Powaski, *The Cold War: The United States and the Soviet Union, 1917–1991* (New York: Oxford University Press, 1998), 212–15.

7 Ralph B. Levering, *The Cold War: A Post-Cold War History* (Wheeling, IL: Harlan-Davidson, 1994), 161.

8 See Odd Arne Westad, "The Road to Kabul: Soviet Policy in Afghanistan, 1978–1979", in *The Fall of Détente*, 118–48.

6 THE RISE AND FALL OF THE SECOND COLD WAR, 1981–91

1 See Ronald Powask, *The Cold War: The United States and the Soviet Union, 1917–1991* (New York: Oxford University Press), 247–49.
2 Raymond L. Garthoff, *The Great Transition: American–Soviet Relations and the End of the Cold War* (Washington, DC: Brookings Institution, 1994), 511.
3 Ibid., 680–81.
4 For references to the debate over Jaruzelski's actions, see ibid., 546n–547n.
5 This account is drawn mainly from ibid., 548–50. Garthoff notes the irony of the United States exerting economic pressure on its allies ostensibly to protect them from Soviet economic pressure.
6 See Michael MccGwire, *Perestroika and Soviet National Security* (Washington, DC: Brookings Institution, 1991); and R. Craig Nation, *Black Earth, Red Star: A History of Soviet Security Policy, 1917–1991* (Ithaca, NY: Cornell University Press, 1992), Chapter 8.
7 There are various versions of this argument; see, for example, John Lewis Gaddis, "Hanging Tough Paid Off," *Bulletin of the Atomic Scientists* 45 (January–February, 1989): 11–14.
8 See Garthoff, *Great Transition*, 751–78; MccGwire, *Perestroika*, 381–93; and Mike Bowker, *Russian Foreign Policy and the End of the Cold War* (Brookfield, VT: Dartmouth Publishing Corporation, 1997).

7 UNDERSTANDING THE COLD WAR

1 Philip Dibb, *The Soviet Union: The Incomplete Superpower*, second edn (London: Macmillan, 1988).
2 As Richard Betts has pointed out, however, parity itself is an elusive concept: "If it meant mutual vulnerability to unacceptable damage, parity came in the mid-1950s; if it meant nearly equal levels of civil damage, it arrived by the early 1970s; if equality in missiles or delivery vehicles, by the mid-1970s; if the measure is the balance of forces as a whole or of counterforce capacity, by the late 1970s." See Richard K. Betts, *Nuclear Blackmail and Nuclear Balance* (Washington, DC: Brookings Institution, 1987), 188.
3 Richard Crockatt, *The Fifty Years War: The United States and the Soviet Union in World Politics* (London: Routledge, 1995), 140.
4 For a similar argument, see Edward H. Judge and John W. Langdon, *A Hard and Bitter Peace: A Global History of the Cold War* (Upper Saddle River, NJ: Prentice-Hall, 1996), 312–13.
5 See William C. Wohlforth, "New Evidence on Moscow's Cold War," *Diplomatic History* 21 (Spring 1997): 229–42.
6 See Thomas G. Paterson, *Soviet–American Confrontation: Postwar Recon-*

struction and the Origins of the Cold War (Baltimore, MD: Johns Hopkins University Press, 1973), 175n. Paterson and others, in particular William Appleman Williams, note that such expansion has been a central theme of US history.

7 On the costs to the United States, see Martin Walker, *The Cold War: A History* (New York: Henry Holt and Company, 1994), chap. 14; and Stephen I. Schwartz, ed. *Atomic Audit: The Costs and Consequences of US Nuclear Weapons Since 1940* (Washington, DC: Brookings Institution, 1998). On the environmental costs to the Soviet Union, see, for example, Murray Feshbach, *Ecological Disaster: Cleaning Up the Hidden Legacy of the Soviet Union* (Washington, DC: Brookings Institution, 1994).

8 I wish to thank my colleague John McNeill for suggesting this phrase.

Suggested further reading

Betts, Richard K. *Nuclear Blackmail and Nuclear Balance*. Washington, DC: Brookings Institution, 1987.

Bowker, Mike and Phil Williams. *Superpower Détente: A Reappraisal*. London: Sage, 1988.

Bright, Charles and Michael Geyer. "For a Unified History of the World in the Twentieth Century." *Radical History Review* 39 (1987): 69–91.

Cohen, Warren I. *America in the Age of Soviet Power, 1945–1991*. Vol. 4 of *The Cambridge History of American Foreign Relations*. New York: Cambridge University Press, 1993.

Cox, Michael. "From the Truman Doctrine to the Second Superpower Détente: The Rise and Fall of the Cold War." *Journal of Peace Research* 27 (February 1990): 25–41.

Crockatt, Richard. *The Fifty Years War: The United States and the Soviet Union in World Politics*. London: Routledge, 1995.

Cronin, James E. *The World the Cold War Made: Order, Chaos, and the Return of History*. London: Routledge, 1996.

Daniels, Robert V. *The End of the Communist Revolution*. London: Routledge, 1993.

Dunbabin, J. P. D. *International Relations since 1945*. Vol. 1: *The Cold War: The Great Powers and their Allies*. Vol. 2: *The Post-imperial Age: The Great Powers and the Wider World*. London: Longman, 1994.

Gaddis, John Lewis. *Strategies of Containment: A Critical Appraisal of Post-war American National Security Policy*. New York: Oxford University Press, 1982.

Garthoff, Raymond L. *Détente and Confrontation: American–Soviet Relations from Nixon to Reagan*. Rev. edn. Washington, DC: Brookings Institution, 1994.

——. *The Great Transition: American–Soviet Relations and the End of the Cold War*. Washington, DC: Brookings Institution, 1994.

Hobsbawm, Eric J. *The Age of Extremes: A History of the World, 1914–1991*. New York: Pantheon Books, 1994.

Hogan, Michael J., ed. *The End of the Cold War: Its Meaning and Implications*. New York: Cambridge University Press, 1992.

——, ed. *America in the World: The Historiography of American Foreign Relations since 1941*. New York: Cambridge University Press, 1995.

Holloway, David. *Stalin and the Bomb: The Soviet Union and Atomic Energy, 1939–56*. New Haven, CT: Yale University Press, 1994.

Jentleson, Bruce W. and Thomas G. Paterson, eds. *Encyclopedia of US Foreign Relations*. 4 vols. New York: Oxford University Press, 1997.

Kennedy, Paul. *The Rise and Fall of the Great Powers: Economic Change and Military Conflict from 1500 to 2000*. New York: Random House, 1987.

Kolko, Gabriel. *Century of War: Politics, Conflict, and Society since 1914*. New York: New Press, 1994.

LaFeber, Walter. *America, Russia, and the Cold War, 1945–1996*. Eighth edn. New York: McGraw-Hill, 1997.

Lebow, Richard Ned and Janice Gross Stein. *We All Lost the Cold War*. Princeton, NJ: Princeton University Press, 1994.

Leffler, Melvyn P. *A Preponderance of Power: National Security, the Truman Administration, and the Cold War*. Stanford, CA: Stanford University Press, 1992.

——. *The Specter of Communism: The United States and the Origins of the Cold War, 1917–1953*. New York: Hill & Wang, 1994.

Leffler, Melvyn P. and David S. Painter, eds. *Origins of the Cold War: An International History*. London: Routledge, 1994.

Levering, Ralph B. *The Cold War: A Post-Cold War History*. Wheeling, IL: Harlan-Davidson, 1994.

MccGwire, Michael. *Perestroika and Soviet National Security*. Washington, DC: Brookings Institution, 1991.

McCormick, Thomas J. *America's Half-century: United States Foreign Policy in the Cold War*. Second edn. Baltimore, MD: Johns Hopkins University Press, 1995.

McMahon, Robert J. and Thomas G. Paterson, eds. *The Origins of the Cold War*. Fourth edn. Boston, MA: Houghton Mifflin, 1999.

Maier, Charles S. *In Search of Stability: Explorations in Historical Political Economy*. New York: Cambridge University Press, 1987.

Martel, Gordon, ed. *American Foreign Relations Reconsidered, 1890–1993*. London: Routledge, 1993.

Nation, R. Craig. *Black Earth, Red Star: A History of Soviet Security Policy, 1917–1991*. Ithaca, NY: Cornell University Press, 1992.

Paterson, Thomas G. *Meeting the Communist Threat: Truman to Reagan*. New York: Oxford University Press, 1988.

Paterson, Thomas G. *On Every Front: The Making and Unmaking of the Cold War*. Rev. edn. New York: W.W. Norton & Company, 1992.

Powaski, Ronald E. *The Cold War: The United States and the Soviet Union, 1917–1991*. New York: Oxford University Press, 1998.

Vadney, T. E. *The World since 1945*. Second edn. Harmondsworth: Penguin, 1992.

Walker, Martin. *The Cold War: A History*. New York: Henry Holt and Company, 1994.

Woodrow Wilson Center. *Cold War International History Project Bulletin*. Vols 1–10. Washington, DC, 1992–98.

Young, John W. *Cold War and Détente, 1941–1991*. London: Longman, 1993.

Zubok, Vladislav and Constantine Pleshakov. *Inside the Kremlin's Cold War: From Stalin to Khrushchev*. Cambridge, MA: Harvard University Press, 1996.

Index